THE MANHATTAN PROJECT

DON E. BEYER

THE MANHATTAN PROJECT

AMERICA MAKES
THE FIRST ATOMIC BOMB

FOREWORD BY
HANS A. BETHE

Barbara Silberdick Feinberg,
Consulting Editor

FRANKLIN WATTS
A TWENTIETH CENTURY
AMERICAN HISTORY BOOK
NEW YORK LONDON TORONTO SYDNEY
1991

For Ray Starrett and his work
toward making a better world.
—D.E.B.

Diagrams by Vantage Art

Excerpts on pages 72–74 were taken from *Hiroshima*
by John Hersey. Copyright 1946 and renewed 1974 by
John Hersey. Reprinted by permission of Alfred A.
Knopf, Inc. Originally appeared in *The New Yorker.*

Library of Congress Cataloging-in-Publication Data

Beyer, Don E.
The Manhattan Project : America makes the first atomic bomb /
by Don E. Beyer.
p.   cm. — (A Twentieth century American history book)
Includes bibliographical references (p.   ) and index.
Summary: Discusses the development and work of the project which
created the first atomic bomb, as well as its devastating effects
and political consequences.
ISBN 0-531-11008-7
1. Atomic bomb—United States—History—Juvenile literature.
2. Manhattan Project (U.S.)—History—Juvenile literature.
[1. Atomic bomb—History.   2. Manhattan Project (U.S.)]
I. Title.   II. Series.
QC773.3.U5B48   1991
355.8'25119'097309044—dc20   90-13049   CIP   AC

CONTENTS

THE MANHATTAN PROJECT

FOREWORD

The atomic bomb changed the world. A few weeks after the two bombs were dropped, Albert Einstein said, "Everything has changed, except the thinking of people."

The atomic bomb brought World War II to an end, saving hundreds of thousands, maybe millions of lives. One should remember, however, that the bomb was not the most important technical invention leading to the victory of the Allies. The most important was radar. Both the Allies and Germany and Japan had radar, but the Allied radar was far superior and won some of the war's decisive battles.

The development of the bomb is told well and vividly in this book. The United States embarked on the development because of fear—fear that Nazi Germany would develop the bomb first. In fact, the Germans had a head start because the underlying scientific fact, the fission of uranium, was discovered by two Germans.

At Los Alamos, I was the leader of the Division of Theoretical Physics. My responsibilities gave me the feeling that I was constantly pushing a big load up a hill. Oppenheimer and General Groves must have had the same feeling even more strongly. Everyone at Los Alamos was strongly aware of his dependence on everyone else.

There had to be teamwork, and Americans have been very successful at teamwork for a long time. Participation in this teamwork, and the conviction that it was important for the war effort, gave us deep satisfaction.

After the war, many efforts were made to establish control over the atomic bomb. The most far-reaching was that of Secretary of State Dean Acheson and David Lilienthal, who developed an elaborate proposal to put atomic weapons under international control. Bernard Baruch presented this to the United Nations, but unfortunately it was rejected by the Soviet Union because it would interfere with their national sovereignty.

The arms race between the Soviet Union and the United States would have happened anyway because there was deep antagonism between East and West. But it was aggravated by the atomic bomb. Whenever one side made some progress, the other side felt that it had to match it. Again it was fear that drove the arms race.

What if the A-bomb had not been made during the war? It would probably have been developed afterwards by one side or the other, in secret. In secret such a weapon is far more dangerous than it is in the open.

Niels Bohr, after Einstein the greatest physicist of the twentieth century, called the atomic bomb "a peril and a hope." For forty-five years we have lived with the peril. It was a shadow over the lives of many of us all over the world. But the statesmen have seen that the atom bomb is not a weapon of war; it has never been used after World War II, although sometimes its use was threatened. By now, I believe that we are living up to Einstein's ideas: man's thinking has indeed begun to change.

The great Soviet statesman Mikhail Gorbachev is leading the way out of the arms race, to arms reduction both in conventional and in atomic weapons. There is hope.

Hans A. Bethe

PROLOGUE
THE DAY EVERYTHING CHANGED

The dark, ugly bulk of Fat Man perched atop the concrete and steel tower 100 feet (30 m) above the desert sands of New Mexico. The countdown began at minus twenty minutes in the rain-washed pre-dawn of Monday, July 16, 1945. The time was 5:09 A.M. Shortly, in a brilliant and frightening explosion, the first atomic bomb would burst upon the world to shake the foundations of human existence.

As the seconds ticked away, some observers looked into the sky with relief. The thunderstorms which had lashed the desert flatland of the Jornada del Muerto (Journey of Death) for hours before had moved on. Here and there a star poked through the overcast.

But some onlookers felt no relief at all, only mounting pressure. The atmosphere was alive with questions. Would the bomb actually explode? Would three years of frantic and secret preparation costing many millions of dollars end in the failure of the world's largest physics experiment? And what if the test succeeded? The effects of an atomic explosion were as yet unknown. None of the Manhattan Project scientists expected serious trouble, yet who could be certain? Enrico Fermi, a senior physicist with the project, attempted to break the tension with black humor.

Joking that the blast would probably ignite the atmosphere, Fermi offered to take bets. Would the explosion destroy only New Mexico or the entire world? Not everyone thought the joke was funny. In a more optimistic vein, some of the scientists organized a betting pool. Pay a dollar and guess the size of the explosion. Bets varied from zero to the equivalent of 45,000 tons of TNT. Jokes and games were the recourse of worried men.

If fear and tension were in the air that early morning of July 16, so was hope. The success of Trinity (the code name for the test of the first atomic bomb) would mean that the United States had sole control of the most powerful weapon ever devised by humankind. Certainly, such terrible power must end the war that still raged in the Pacific and make a costly invasion of the Japanese homelands unnecessary. What enemy could refuse to surrender when confronted with The Bomb? The greatest instrument of destruction would bring peace. Such hopes rode on the ticks of the clock as zero hour approached.

Twenty miles (32 km) from the explosion center, or ground zero, another group of observers shared the tension of the countdown by passing around suntan lotion. In the early morning darkness, they coated their faces and hands as protection against the intense light flash of the explosion. Others prepared to view the event through sunglasses and pieces of welder's glass. They heard the countdown broadcast over shortwave radio.

Five miles (8 km) away from the bomb, the command center was crowded. A scientist nervously stood before a switch, ready to halt the explosion if something went wrong. Dr. Robert Oppenheimer, director of the laboratory at Los Alamos, New Mexico, which made the bomb, stared quietly in the direction of ground zero. The last few seconds seemed unbearably long.

Five. Four. Three. Two. One. Zero.

Fat Man exploded.

In just millionths of a second, an atomic chain reaction released an energy force equivalent to over 17,000 tons of conventional explosives (TNT). The heat generated at the center of the explosion rose to four times the hottest temperature of the sun. For two seconds, night turned to brightest day in an enormous blinding flash of light. An accompanying air blast knocked down observers 5 miles (8 km) away. The sound rolled over the desert like a tidal wave. A great seething ball of fire—blue, purple, yellow, scarlet, green—rose into the air in awesome majesty. It swirled sand, debris, and smoke into a huge mushroom-shaped radioactive cloud, the signature of an atomic blast, which climbed 42,000 feet (12,800 m) into the New Mexico sky.

Then and later, eyewitnesses struggled to understand and describe this terrible power that had been unleashed into the world. For one person, the spectacle was an apocalyptic vision from the Bible's Book of Revelations. Another, Robert Oppenheimer, was reminded of lines from the Hindu classic, *The Bhagavad-Gita:* "Now I am become Death, the destroyer of worlds."[1] Some people cried. A few laughed. Most were shocked into quiet. The blast, heard 100 miles (160 km) away, was visible at a distance of 180 miles (290 km). At ground zero it vaporized the steel and concrete tower that had held the bomb and created a crater 1,200 feet (366 m) across. The sands around were fused into green glass. For a half mile (.8 km) around the blast center, radiation killed all desert animals not hidden deeply underground.

In a matter of hours the smoke of the giant mushroom cloud had cleared. Once more the desert was quiet. Those far away from the testing ground who had seen or heard evidence of the blast and asked questions were given an official story to cover the top secret event. A stockpile of explosives had gone off accidentally at the Air Force testing range at Alamogordo, they were told. Nothing to worry about. Business as usual.

If nothing seemed very different to most people on that July morning, the fact is everything had changed. An incredibly powerful and frightening nuclear genie had been let out of the bottle. The Nuclear Age had begun. For the first time, human beings had invented a means of death, a nuclear Sword of Damocles, that could destroy millions of their kind, and all manner of living things, in less time than it takes to watch the late movie. The Trinity explosion of July 1945 is a symbol of that potential for self-destruction.

Though the United States was the first country to develop and use the atom bomb, the knowledge of how to make such a weapon could not be kept secret for very long. When the Soviet Union became the world's second nuclear power, an arms race began that continues to this day. Trying to ensure peace by building greater and more destructive weapons of war, creating what Winston Churchill called a "balance of terror," has become a way of life. It has spawned a self-perpetuating network—a military-industrial complex—devoted to creating nuclear weapons that has flourished in an unsteady atmosphere of nervous peace, a kind of "Pax Atomica," for more than forty years.

It is estimated that there are 50,000 or more nuclear weapons in existence today in the arsenals of eight or so nations. The superpowers, the United States and the Soviet Union, have aimed most of these at one another. If a sufficient number of such weapons were to be unleashed upon the world, their power would probably rend the complex fabric of civilization and kill most human beings in the process. This ugly fact is made worse when one considers the cost of creating such destructive potential.

Trillions of dollars have been spent on the development of nuclear arsenals and delivery systems. The expenditure of much of this money has diminished the world's standard of living. Jobs, economic growth, and social programs designed to lessen human suffering have been sacrificed. The horrendous cost of trying to stay ahead in the nuclear arms race has contributed significantly to the current economic problems, reflected in great budget deficits, of both the Soviet Union and the United States. But there are other human costs which can't always be expressed in dollars and cents.

The psychological effects of living with nuclear weapons have also been considerable. Generations have grown up in the shadow of the mushroom cloud, an atmosphere of fear, insecurity, and tension. Some researchers believe that many people have repressed or hidden their fear of extinction in a nuclear war, and that this has resulted in a condition called "psychic numbing," or loss of sensitivity to other aspects of life. [2] Others have lost their faith in the future. In a 1984 Gallup survey, 75 percent of all women and 78 percent of all people under thirty believed that "if we and the Soviets keep building missiles instead of negotiating to get rid of them, it's only a matter of time before they are used." [3] Despair about the future may have impacted even more on the young. The Nuclear Ecology Research Project, which has studied the effects of the nuclear threat on both American and Soviet children, has warned that "we are facing a mental health problem of epidemic proportions." [4]

On the other side of the issue, the splitting of the atom and the release of nuclear power has been used to benefit humanity. Nuclear power plants, though not without their own special set of problems, generate electricity to meet growing demands. Through the technology of nuclear medicine, thousands of lives are saved each year, especially in the treatment of cancer. Continued research in the area of nuclear energy will yield even more knowledge about the world, much of which may find useful applications for people. Like many human endeavors, the harnessing of nuclear energy may be turned to good or bad use. Yet the dark side of its application, in the form of devastating weapons of war, may make the good irrelevant.

Many of the people who witnessed the first test of the atomic bomb came to understand this dilemma. The Trinity test at Alamogordo, New Mexico, in July 1945 marked the beginning of the era of nuclear weapons. How and why it came about is the story of the Manhattan Project.

I

THE ROAD TO MANHATTAN

The story of the Manhattan Project and the atomic bomb opens with a series of new discoveries in physics that began near the turn of the century. The term classical is applied to the physics that scientists developed prior to that time. Much of it came from the work of the Father of Physics, the great seventeenth-century English scholar, Sir Isaac Newton. Newton was a scientific genius. Today, however, a competent student with a good high school or college physics course probably has a more accurate knowledge of the physical universe than Newton had. This is especially true concerning the most basic building blocks of matter, atoms and their components called subatomic particles.

Newton, as did others before him, developed a theory about the structure of atoms. The idea that atoms were the building blocks of matter is very old, originating in Greece during the fifth century B.C. By Newton's time scientists had proposed and discussed a variety of atomic models. According to Newton's pet theory, atoms were like marbles. They were solid and hard, but, unlike marbles, they could not be further divided. It was not until the latter half of the nineteenth century that scientific experiment began to prove otherwise. Thereafter, knowledge of atomic structure moved ahead very quickly.

By the mid-1930s, dedicated effort by British and other European scientists had revealed a new world of atomic structure. The atom was not marblelike and indivisible as Newton had thought, but rather an incredibly tiny system of interacting subatomic particles: electrons, protons, and neutrons. At the center of the atom was the nucleus, composed of positively charged protons and neutrons with no electrical charge. This nuclear core contained most of the weight and bulk of the atom. Around it orbited one or more negatively charged electrons. But how all the parts of the atom were held together was a mystery.

According to classical or Newtonian physics, the relationship of subatomic particles was unstable and, at least in theory, the atom should not hold together. The negatively charged electrons must either go whizzing off away from the positively charged nucleus or crash into it, depending on the number of electrons involved. Yet the atom certainly appeared to be an extremely stable structure. Theory did not agree with scientific observation. Niels Bohr, a young and brilliant Danish physicist, broke through the apparent contradiction.

Bohr built on the work of German scientists Max Planck and Albert Einstein to show that classical physics—the Newtonian model which applies to large scale events like the movement of planets—did not work at the atomic level. Electrons and nuclei just don't behave in the way that planets do. Bohr used a newly emerging branch of physics, quantum theory, to explain why and how electrons could remain in a stable orbit around the atom's nucleus. This work on an atomic model that broke with the traditions of classical physics earned Bohr the Nobel Prize in physics in 1922.

The energy required to hold subatomic particles together inside the atom became a source of continued interest and speculation as physics developed in the twentieth century. Working in Switzerland in 1905, the brilliant theoretical physicist Albert Einstein developed the famous equation $E=mc^2$ (energy equals mass times the speed of light squared) and characterized all matter as frozen energy. The potential was staggering. If the energy in just a single ounce (28 g) of matter could be released at one time, the resulting explosion would be equivalent to the detonation of millions of tons of TNT. But could it be done?

Many scientists believed the whole idea of converting matter to energy by the disintegration of the atom was unlikely and belonged more to the realm of science fiction than science. Both Einstein and the British physicist Ernest Rutherford, leaders in the scientific community, were skeptical. Rutherford called the idea "moonshine" or nonsense. "[W]e cannot control atomic energy," he said, "to an extent [that] would be of any value commercially, and I believe we are not likely ever to be able to do so."[1] Yet the prospect was tantalizing. A seemingly unlimited supply of energy was available in the atom, if only it could be tapped. It was the stuff of dreams.

One scientist, Leo Szilard, was both a theoretical physicist and a dreamer. Szilard pursued engineering studies in his native Hungary but switched to physics after moving to Berlin in 1919 and being exposed to the work of world-class physicists Albert Einstein, Max Planck, and Max von Laue. Original and imaginative work in a branch of physics called thermodynamics earned Szilard a doctor's degree in 1925 from the University of Berlin. He stayed on as a visiting teacher and scholar until 1933, when German political violence and growing anti-Semitism convinced him that Berlin was not a healthy environment for a Hungarian Jew. He got out just in time and made his way to England. In England Szilard devoted much of his time to thinking about the power locked inside the atom—

what Einstein had called frozen energy—and how it might benefit humankind.

The discovery of the neutron particle in 1932 stimulated Szilard to wonder about how the binding energy of the atomic nucleus, the force which held neutrons and protons together, might be released in a process called chain reaction. The neutron, he reasoned, because it had no electrical charge, could be used to blast an atom's nucleus, causing it to disintegrate and release both energy and more neutrons (see diagram below). These would in turn repeat the process with still more nuclei in a quickly growing reaction called an exponential (1,3,9,27, etc.) chain.

In 1939, Szilard developed an experiment which showed that a chain reaction was indeed possible. But only if such a reaction could be kept going, he reasoned, could the energy released be useful. Szilard, and other scientists

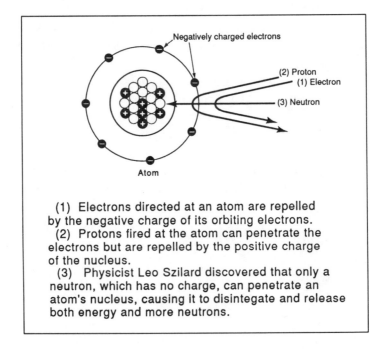

Negatively charged electrons

(2) Proton
(1) Electron
(3) Neutron

Atom

(1) Electrons directed at an atom are repelled by the negative charge of its orbiting electrons.
(2) Protons fired at the atom can penetrate the electrons but are repelled by the positive charge of the nucleus.
(3) Physicist Leo Szilard discovered that only a neutron, which has no charge, can penetrate an atom's nucleus, causing it to disintegate and release both energy and more neutrons.

in Europe and America, continued experimenting with the neutron to probe the secrets and possibilities of nuclear energy. The work moved ahead slowly. Then a startling breakthrough occurred.

Working independently, physicist Enrico Fermi in Rome and the team of Otto Hahn and Fritz Strassmann in Berlin experimented with the neutron bombardment of uranium. The work produced a variety of radioactive substances, some of which could not be immediately identified. What scientists were seeing but not understanding was something completely new to them, the splitting of the uranium nucleus into two parts to form different elements. Puzzling over the Hahn-Strassmann results, physicists Lise Meitner and Otto Frisch identified and explained the splitting process and showed that it was accompanied by a tremendous release of energy. Frisch gave it the name fission (from the Latin word meaning to split).

The news of this discovery electrified the scientific community. The effect, Leo Szilard was to recall later, was like poking a stick into an ants' nest.[2] Scientists in Europe and America rushed to their laboratories to study the fission process. But, amidst all the scientific excitement, Szilard was worried. The fission breakthrough rekindled his belief in the possibility of a sustainable chain reaction and the use of the great quantities of energy it would release. While he hoped that such energy might be used for the benefit of society, he also envisioned its destructive potential in the form of an atomic bomb. What if such a power should fall into the wrong hands? Szilard knew firsthand the violent and hate-filled atmosphere of Nazi Germany. He believed he had good reason to worry.

THE RACE FOR THE ATOMIC BOMB

While physicists eagerly developed new lines of research in the wake of the discovery of nuclear fission in 1938, Europe was moving toward war. In Germany, Adolf Hitler's ominous star had been on the rise since 1933. Fear of German aggression was the stimulus for atomic bomb development in Great Britain and America. Ironically, Hitler's dedicated program of anti-Semitism made exiles of hundreds of Jewish scientists. Many of these scientists eventually became political refugees who contributed greatly to the success of the Manhattan Project.

Adolf Hitler came to power in a Germany infected by fear, economic despair, and growing resentment. In the years between the World Wars, inflation and then depression brought the German economy to near ruin. Unemployment was widespread and food supplies were often inadequate to meet the needs of a hungry nation. Resentment grew as the victorious Allied powers demanded reparations for war damages from a nation unable to pay. The democratic Weimar Republic, hated and attacked by a powerful and vocal minority, was helpless to cope with growing economic, social, and political unrest. Onto this turbulent national stage stepped Adolf Hitler.

Ever the opportunist, Hitler climbed from obscurity to

build on German fears and preach a gospel of national pride and hatred of those he characterized as enemies of the true German people. The National Socialist (Nazi) Party rose to prominence in the early 1930s on a platform of anti-communism. Hitler used his considerable skills as an orator and propagandist to convince many that he could save the German people.

"Der Fuehrer" (the Leader), as Hitler came to be called, targeted Jews as scapegoats. In the poisonous language of hatred, his book, Mein Kampf (My Struggle), reviled them and claimed the existence of a Jewish conspiracy to dominate the world. The Jews, he screamed to his followers at huge rallies, were responsible for the ills and sufferings of the German people. Get rid of the Jews, he insisted, and Germany would assert its rightful place in world affairs.

Though he was briefly imprisoned for political agitation, Hitler used his popularity and bullying tactics to assume legal public office. He became the chancellor of Germany in 1933. Soon thereafter his program of anti-Semitism became law and the government abolished the civil rights of German Jews. As persecution intensified, Jewish scientists lost their positions in government and in universities, both within Germany and in those nations which later fell under the German yoke. Many escaped in a brain-drain important to the Allied cause. In the United States alone, nearly one hundred physicists found safety from Nazi persecution as political refugees.

Having consolidated his position at home, Hitler turned his attention to the acquisition of neighboring lands. Violating the Treaty of Versailles, he occupied the Rhineland, and then took Austria and much of Czechoslovakia, claiming that these territories with large German populations were rightfully part of the "Fatherland." Rather than risk another war, France and Great Britain chose to appease Hitler by allowing German expansion. On September 1, 1939, confident of German military power and emboldened by the lack of resistance from the other European powers, Hitler invaded Poland in a lightning air and tank attack called the "blitzkrieg." Great Britain and France declared war immediately. America looked on with concern and disgust.

In its early years, World War II was only a European war to most Americans. The horrors of World War I, the mass death and destruction, were still vivid memories. Isolationism, the feeling that Europeans should deal with their own messes without American involvement, was widespread. Prominent American isolationists, like Charles A. Lindbergh who represented the America First Committee, claimed that "more than 80 percent" of Americans opposed U.S. entry into the war.[1] Those in government who believed in the inevitability, or at least the likelihood, of America's entry into the war, could not make preparations openly in the prevailing atmosphere of isolationism. Neither could they allow the country to be completely unprepared should war occur. President Franklin Delano Roosevelt (FDR) was in a difficult position and had to move cautiously. Peacetime financial resources for the military were severely limited and could be used to fund only the most promising weapons programs. At that time, almost no one believed in the promise of nuclear energy for creating weapons.

In the late 1930s, even with the successful demonstration of nuclear fission by Hahn and Strassmann, few physicists were willing to step forward as advocates of government-sponsored nuclear weapons research. Most believed, in fact, that immense scientific and technical problems made the practical use of nuclear fission unlikely for either peaceful or military purposes. But a few scientists strongly disagreed.

Leo Szilard, together with his longtime friends and fellow Hungarian physicists Eugene Wigner and Edward Teller, agreed that the president must be warned; fission bomb technology was not so farfetched. The Jewish emigrés, now living in America, had personal experience of fascism in Europe. Deeply concerned, they believed that the possibility of hostile nations creating atomic weapons had to be faced. The American government, especially the president as military commander in chief and head policy maker, had to be convinced that the money and effort needed for the search for atomic weapons was worthwhile and essential. But how could they get the president to listen?

In 1939 the three physicists enlisted the support of Albert Einstein, the most famous scientist of his day, whose personal integrity and brilliance as a theoretical physicist were esteemed. They used Einstein's reputation to gain the president's attention. The four men met at Einstein's summer home on Long Island and drafted a letter to Roosevelt stating that "uranium may be turned into a new and important source of energy in the immediate future" and calling "for watchfulness and, if necessary, quick action on the part of the administration." The letter went on to warn that nuclear fission "would . . . lead to the construction of bombs, and it is conceivable—though much less certain—that extremely powerful bombs of a new type may thus be constructed."[2] The letter, dated August 2, was signed by Einstein and entrusted to Alexander Sachs, an economist and FDR supporter who had the ear of the president. Sachs delivered the letter on October 11. Hitler's invasion of Poland only a month before gave added weight to the concerns expressed in the Einstein message.

When Sachs met the president, he opened with a story, a kind of parable to fit the occasion. An American engineer, Sachs told FDR, approached the French Emperor Napoleon with a proposal to build a fleet of steam-powered ships, an all-weather fleet, which could be used to attack England. Napoleon snorted in disbelief. How could ships possibly move without sails? He ridiculed and rejected the inventor's ideas. That engineer, Sachs told the president dramatically, was none other than Robert Fulton, inventor of the steamboat. [3]

Sachs then summarized the contents of the Einstein letter. He talked about the possibilities of using atomic energy for both peaceful and destructive purposes, but especially as bombs, and warned of the consequences of such weapons in the hands of a hostile power. Given recent events in Europe, hostile power meant Nazi Germany. The warning was clearly understood by the president. "Pa," he told his attaché, General "Pa" Watson, "this requires action!"[4] With FDR's initial rush of enthusiasm, it appeared that a strong atomic weapons research program was about to become a reality. Szilard, Wigner, and Teller, the ghostwriters of the Einstein letter, were elated.

Within days of his meeting with Sachs, the president appointed a three-person group, the Advisory Committee on Uranium, to study the possibilities of using atomic energy for national defense. Dr. Lyman J. Briggs, a long-time government scientist and director of the Bureau of Standards, was picked to head the Uranium Committee whose other members represented the Army and Navy. Briggs invited the three Hungarian physicists to attend the committee's first meeting on October 31, 1939. There Szilard explained ideas on producing a chain reaction in uranium and also estimated the destructive force of an atomic bomb. The first report of the Advisory Committee on Uranium, issued November 1, 1939, recommended to the president that financial support be given for research on a controlled chain reaction. Then, following the first flurry of activity, the progress of the Uranium Committee slowed to a crawl, much to the dismay of worried emigrant scientists.

President Roosevelt, caught up in the serious affairs of the European war, delegated the largely scientific work of the Uranium Committee to Lyman Briggs. Briggs had a conservative leadership style. He needed good reasons for backing a particular course of action and did not share the sense of urgency, felt by Szilard, Wigner, and Teller, that was prompted by fears of what might be happening in German laboratories. From Briggs's point of view there seemed to be good reason for the Uranium Committee to proceed slowly and cautiously. The United States was not at war. And even if the country did go to war, Briggs reasoned, scientists could not offer assurances that military applications of atomic fission were likely to be forthcoming in the near future. In fact, some influential American scientists, unlike their emigré counterparts, still had serious doubts that fission would ever prove useful.

It was evident that a serious commitment to fission bomb research would never occur until senior policy makers took more interest. The people at the top needed to be convinced that such weapons were needed, that they would work well, and that somebody could make them fairly quickly. Yet no one was willing to say without serious reservations that any of these conditions could be met. Thus, as America's friends struggled for survival in Europe and as events moved the United States closer to war, the program that sought to harness the energy of the atom inched along with little energy of its own. By late 1940, less than $50,000 had been allocated for bomb-related research.[5] Efforts to explore the explosive potential of nuclear fission were still relegated to the back burner of the administrative stove. The events of 1941 changed that. The first stimulus came from Great Britain.

Fission research in Great Britain was also proceeding

slowly because of significant doubts about the possibility of making bombs. The work of two emigré scientists, Otto Frisch and Rudolph Peierls, changed the minds of British policy makers and directly influenced American military priorities. When war broke out in Europe, Otto Frisch was in England visiting Mark Oliphant, head of the physics department at Birmingham, who was engaged in war-related work. Fearing that Denmark might soon fall to Hitler, Frisch decided not to return to his position at the Bohr Institute in Copenhagen. He found important work to do in England. Collaborating with Peierls, a German physicist who had been in England since 1933, Frisch pursued the possibility of using fast neutrons for the fission of U-235, a naturally occurring isotope of uranium, at a time when American scientists were investigating the potential for fission by slow neutrons. Frisch and Peierls sought answers to several key questions: Was the fission of U-235 by fast neutrons actually possible? If so, how strong was this fission process? Could enough U-235 be separated from natural uranium to make it work in a bomb? How much would be needed?

The answers to these questions, worked out in the spring of 1941, formed the basis of a report by a British committee, code-named MAUD, organized to review the potential for atomic bomb development. The conclusions of the MAUD Report were bold and disturbing. It maintained that the development of an atomic bomb fueled by U-235 was not only possible but could be completed in a minimum of three years. Furthermore, the destructive potential of such a bomb was tremendous and was "likely to lead to decisive results in the war." Facilities to separate enough U-235 to fuel a production line of bombs could be constructed at an estimated cost of £5,000,000. In recommending "the highest priority" for a bomb project, even if the war should end before bombs were ready, the MAUD

Report foresaw the significance of atomic weapons in the postwar future.[6]

Though the MAUD Report was not officially released until October 1941, copies of a draft were in the hands of key American administrators several months earlier. Yet the British heard nothing in response. When Mark Oliphant flew to the United States on wartime business in August of that year, he was charged with finding out why the Americans seemed to be ignoring the vital information of the report. He was disturbed to learn that the MAUD Report was sitting in Lyman Briggs's safe and that the cautious Briggs had not even shared it with the other members of the Uranium Committee. Oliphant attended a meeting of the Uranium Committee in late August where he criticized American foot-dragging and stated in unambiguous terms that an atomic bomb project must become a priority. The weight of the British MAUD Report and urgent voices at home finally convinced key American scientists and administrators that the United States must commit to building the bomb. When an official copy of the MAUD Report reached President Roosevelt in October 1941, the president acted.

Roosevelt, advised by Vannevar Bush, who headed the National Defense Research Committee (NDRC), and Vice President Henry Wallace, made the policy decision that moved American atomic bomb research to the forefront of national concerns. His first action was to replace the plodding Advisory Committee on Uranium with a new administrative structure, a Top Policy Group, charged with supervising bomb-related research and reporting directly to the White House. Officially designated Section-1 of the Office of Scientific Research and Development (OSRD), the Top Policy Group consisted of men in the upper levels of national defense work: Vice President Henry Wallace, Secretary of War Henry Stimson, Army

Chief of Staff George C. Marshall, new OSRD Director Vannevar Bush, and recently appointed chairman of the NDRC, James B. Conant. The group met in November 1941 to reorganize the work of the Uranium Committee and to authorize specific projects at centers around the country: gas diffusion separation of U-235 (Columbia University in New York); electromagnetic separation of U-235 (University of California at Berkeley); and chain reaction and bomb design (University of Chicago). The pace of U.S. atomic bomb research had picked up significantly. Mounting fears that Germany was winning the war in Europe moved it along even faster.

Woven into the fabric of the growing fission research program in America was anxiety over Germany's progress toward developing its own atomic bomb. Emigré scientists in Great Britain and America, especially those who had lived and worked in Germany, knew that German physicists could carry out nuclear research at the highest level of competence. It was a race and, given the slow start of bomb research in America, many concerned scientists believed that the Germans were running ahead. Since no one actually knew the rate of progress achieved by German scientists, they tended to believe the worst. There was good reason for concern. In the early months of the war, a German program designed to exploit the military potential of nuclear fission seemed well under way.

Very soon into the war, fission research in Germany was taken over by a department of the War Office and supervised by two physicists, Kurt Diebner and Eric Bagge. The Germans had some strong advantages in the pursuit of a fission bomb. In addition to excellent scientific talent for research, Germany had first-rate industrial facilities and the engineering talent to implement the results of research. Furthermore, access to the Belgian Congo ensured scientists a steady supply of uranium ore. Fortunately for the Allied cause, Germany did not capitalize on its advantages.

As the war raged on and the German economy was stretched to its limit, reservations about fission bomb research began to surface as they had in both Great Britain and America. Only the most promising weapons systems, those that offered important results in a short period of time, could be funded. Top German policy makers were never made to believe that the atomic bomb was worth pursuing in an all-out effort. Other pet projects, especially the V-series rocket program, were considered more important. As a result, by the end of 1942, the German atomic bomb program had fizzled. The Allies were not to learn this until near the very end of the war when a belated intelligence-gathering effort, code-named the ALSOS Mission, captured German scientists and research facilities. Until then, they were driven by the gnawing fear that Germany was ahead in the race for the atomic bomb. With the eye of imagination, they could see those German atomic bombs falling on England and America.

3

BLUEPRINT FOR A BOMB

Americans were shocked when France fell to Hitler in June 1940. Mounting concern over German gains in Europe and sympathy for the plight of Great Britain, pounded day and night by bombing raids, edged the United States away from its isolationist neutrality and closer to the brink of war.

Japan pushed America over the edge. In the early-morning quiet of Sunday, December 7, 1941, more than 250 Japanese carrier-based planes attacked the American naval base at Pearl Harbor, Hawaii. Minutes later, much of the U.S. Pacific Fleet lay twisted and burning or sunk. America responded with a declaration of war against Japan on December 8. Germany and Italy then declared war on the United States, which answered in kind. What for many Americans had started as just another European war suddenly became a full-fledged global conflict.

While the United States government had made its decision to pursue an atomic bomb research program before Pearl Harbor, the Japanese attack and America's entry into the war gave that program additional urgency. More and more scientists and administrators became convinced that a successful bomb program would make a decisive difference in the outcome of the war.

Through 1941 and 1942 most bomb work was basic research carried on by the scientists at university centers—Columbia, Princeton, Berkeley, and Chicago. A key project was the creation of a self-sustaining fission chain reaction to demonstrate the central physical process that would make an atomic bomb work. Creating a successful chain reaction took on added significance when a new element, plutonium, was identified by Glenn Seaborg and Emilio Segrè at Berkeley. Plutonium, which promised to make an excellent bomb fuel, was a by-product of fission chain reactions and could be separated chemically from uranium. In early 1942, administrators consolidated chain reaction and plutonium chemistry research at one center, the Chicago Metallurgical Laboratory (Met Lab). At the Met Lab Enrico Fermi's team continued the chain reaction work started earlier at Columbia. Glenn Seaborg came from Berkeley to pursue the task of isolating the plutonium produced by Fermi's chain reaction.

At Columbia, Fermi had established through laborious experimentation the quantity of uranium (critical mass) and other materials required to sustain a slow-neutron chain reaction. Fermi gave this carefully calculated volume the unromantic name "pile," which became part of the early standard jargon for chain reaction work.

Construction of the first atomic pile began on November 16, 1942, in an unused and unheated doubles squash court beneath a football stadium, Stagg Field, on the University of Chicago campus. It was not the ideal site. Scientists were concerned about conducting such a large-scale and potentially dangerous physics experiment in the heart of a big city. A runaway chain reaction would release lethal radiation and might result in an explosion. Though the scientists believed that a catastrophe was highly unlikely, they did not tell the university administrators about the experiment and its potential dangers. The people of

Chicago carried on their lives oblivious to the unusual happenings in the catacombs of Stagg Field.

The first nuclear pile was an ugly affair, a large, roughly elliptical mass of dark graphite with surrounding timber scaffolding. Layer by layer, workers alternated blocks of solid, neutron-slowing graphite with graphite bricks drilled to take two 5-pound (2.3-kg) uranium pellets. At key places, scientists incorporated slotted bricks of graphite to form channels for control rods of cadmium-covered wood. The rods ran into the heart of the pile. Cadmium, an absorber of neutrons, kept the fission process in check as the pile grew to critical size. Throughout the construction process, Fermi and his co-workers monitored the pile's reactivity, its level of neutron release. It was getting hotter. At the end of each day's work, all control rods were padlocked into place for security.

A self-sustaining chain-reacting pile began as a pristine idea in the minds of scientists. The physical realization of their idea, a structure of slippery graphite bricks, was the product of hard, back-straining, toe-smashing labor in the cold Chicago winter of 1942. The air of the squash court was filled with a graphite haze. Residue from the blocks covered everything, including the men who shifted them one by one.

On December 2, just seventeen days after construction began, the pile was ready for the final phase of the experiment officially named CP-1 (Chicago Pile Number One). The roughly ellipsoid pile with its irregular outer shell stood 25 feet (7.6 m) wide at the equator, 20 feet (6.1 m) high at the poles, and contained over 43 tons of graphite, uranium oxide, and natural uranium in fifty-seven layers.

Above the pile, the balcony of the squash court was filled with about twenty people (including physicist Leona Wood, the only woman directly involved in the pile construction project) and equipment. On the scaffolding around the pile, scientists stood ready to use control rods and cadmium solution to arrest the process of fission should something go wrong. Those closest to the pile were jokingly called the "suicide squad." Fermi gave the order to begin withdrawing the control rods. Neutron counters clicked away with increasing speed as the rods were inched out. The process took most of the morning. At each stage Fermi used a small slide rule to check the levels of energy release in the pile against his calculations. By midafternoon the last control rod was removed from the pile to a length of 8 feet (2.4 m). Then the pile went critical; the fission reaction became self-sustaining and would continue to grow on its own. Left unchecked with all control rods removed, it would run away, killing everyone in the room and releasing deadly radiation into the air of Chicago. The clicking of the neutron counter blurred into a scream as the machine could no longer effectively monitor the exponential growth rate of energy inside the pile. The counter was turned off and the last moments of the experiment were conducted in silence. The pile continued to run for four and a half minutes before Fermi gave the order to shut down. Where others had stood to watch squash games, a select team of scientists had just witnessed the first self-sustaining nuclear chain reaction.

The successful conclusion of CP-1 was a milestone in the development of the American atomic bomb program. It marked the end of the transition from research to development. A self-sustaining chain reaction, the central process of an atomic bomb, had been demonstrated. Though it still remained to be shown that such a chain reaction was possible in the form of a bomb, such an accomplishment seemed well within reach. Very soon, activity would shift away from the academic research facilities like the University of Chicago to applied research and production centers for the actual creation of an atomic bomb and the material to fuel it.

By mid-1942 the atomic bomb program was moving

from a position of relative obscurity and minimal funding under the lethargic Uranium Advisory Committee to its eventual position at the top of wartime priorities with a $2 billion bankroll. As head of OSRD, Vannevar Bush obtained the consent of President Roosevelt to place bomb development and production in the hands of the Army, but with joint military-civilian supervision. The U.S. Army Corps of Engineers (COE) received the assignment to build and run the production facilities needed to make bombs. The Corps selected Col. James C. Marshall to begin that process. Marshall chose the large engineering corporation of Stone and Webster as the main contractor for the bomb program. The Boston-based firm had responsibility for building production facilities wherever they might be needed. The placement of Marshall's office in Manhattan, near the site of early bomb work at Columbia University, led to the selection of the cover name for the bomb program—the Manhattan Engineer District. It soon became the Manhattan Project. Despite Marshall's efforts, the organization of actual atomic bomb production was still just inching along in the fall of 1942 when Colonel (soon to be Brigadier General) Leslie R. Groves of the Army Corps of Engineers was tapped to head the Manhattan Project as officer in charge.

Groves was angry about the new assignment. A career officer in the Engineers since graduating fourth in his class at West Point in 1918, he had just finished building the Pentagon in Washington, D.C., and was itching for an overseas combat assignment. Groves did not relish the idea of staying at home to organize the efforts of civilian scientists (a collection of "crackpots," he was said to have called them[1]) in a program whose ability to influence the outcome of the war he at first doubted. But he soon warmed to the challenge of the assignment.

General Groves was a big man, both in girth and in

ego. Standing just under 6 feet tall and weighing between 250 and 300 pounds, the soldier with a passion for chocolate had a reputation for throwing his weight around to get jobs done. At times abrasive and offensive in his directness, Groves turned out to be the ideal leader for the unusual collection of people and the tangled administrative structure that was the Manhattan Project. He did not inspire love in those around him, but his ability to produce results under difficult circumstances often earned their grudging respect. His procurement officer, Lt. Col. Kenneth D. Nichols, called him "the biggest [SOB] I have ever met in my life, but also one of the most capable individuals."[2]

With General Groves as officer in charge, the Manhattan Project began to move forward with new energy. In just the first few weeks of his appointment, Groves acted with impressive efficiency. To open the necessary bureaucratic doors for the acquisition of materials and manpower, he pushed through priority status for the Manhattan Project with the War Production Board. Groves then arranged the purchase of an important stock of uranium ore from Belgian sources, and purchased land in Tennessee for a bomb fuel production site.

Soon Groves, Vannevar Bush, and James Bryant Conant became the key figures in the management of the Manhattan Project, the men with direct access to the White House who were responsible for carrying out FDR's directives. Bush, as director of the Office of Scientific Research and Development, was in charge. Conant worked closely with Bush and became the unofficial and influential science advisor to Groves. Groves, who accepted more and more responsibility for the Manhattan Project as it continued to develop, mainly supervised the project's engineering phases across the country.

A three-man Military Policy Committee (MPC) created and chaired by Bush became the supervisory authority for the Manhattan Project and the group to which Groves reported on his activities. Though not an official member of the committee, James Bryant Conant attended all meetings. Project scientists hoped that the presence of Bush and Conant, civilians with science backgrounds, would insure the representation of their views as a balance to the military point of view.

From late 1942 the focus of the Manhattan Project was the translation of bomb research into bomb production. Development of facilities, including huge factories and power plants, went on simultaneously at three widely spaced sites across the country: Oak Ridge, Tennessee, for the production of the bomb fuel U-235; Hanford, Washington, for the production of plutonium fuel; and Los Alamos, New Mexico, for bomb production and assembly. Often work proceeded in a vacuum of information, without knowledge of the exact requirements for the installation and operation of machines and processes which were themselves in a state of development. The technology of fission bomb production was so new that no one clearly understood what might be needed. Scientists and engineers were often forced to invent, develop, and improvise as they went along. The Manhattan Project was a gigantic scientific and technological undertaking. The weaving together of such vast quantities of ideas, machines, industrial processes, manpower, and money in so short a time was unprecedented in world history.

The central facility of the Manhattan Project, Los Alamos, grew out of the site of a boys' school in New Mexico. It became the enormous think tank and laboratory that gave birth to the first atomic bombs. Set on a hot and arid mesa (a small, high plateau with steep sides) approximately 35 miles (56 km) northwest of Santa Fe, the school site satisfied General Groves's requirements for the location of the ultrasecret project: adequate transportation and water supply, a ready labor force, moderate climate to enable year-round work, and, of paramount importance, isolation for safety and security. It also commanded a panoramic view of a wild and beautiful terrain of mountains and desert, an important aesthetic consideration for Los Alamos Laboratory director Robert Oppenheimer, who loved and knew the mountain country of New Mexico well. This location, said fellow physicist Victor Weisskopf, with "its romantic isolation in the midst of Indian culture" had a special appeal for Oppenheimer. [3]

Oppenheimer's responsibility as director was to see to the design and production of a workable and practical atomic bomb. He had to accomplish this by the time that fissionable materials, U-235 and plutonium, were available in sufficient quantities, which was expected to take about two years. It was a terrible responsibility, made heavier by the vast quantities of precious wartime resources invested in the project and expectations that a successful atomic bomb would shorten the war and save lives.

An honors graduate of Harvard, Oppenheimer had worked with distinguished scientists in England, Germany, and Holland, specializing in the branch of physics called quantum theory. Between 1926 and 1929 he published sixteen scientific papers which established his credentials and reputation as a theoretical physicist. The young Oppenheimer had a brilliant but troubled mind. His wide-ranging interests—science, literature, Eastern religion, languages—were solitary pursuits. Oppenheimer was not much interested in social causes until the late 1930s, when anti-Semitism in Germany (he had Jewish relatives there) and the effects of the Great Depression on the lives of his students at the California Institute of Technology (Cal tech) and Berkeley were thrust into his awareness. Through his first fiancée, Jean Tatlock, who was a Communist Party member, Oppenheimer became involved in left-wing causes. Others close to him, including Katherine (Kitty) Puening, his future wife, also had Communist Party ties. Though Oppenheimer claimed to have rejected communist ideology, those personal connections were to prove troublesome and damaging to Oppenheimer's career and relationship with the United States government throughout the life of the Manhattan Project and beyond. Always under suspicion by Army Intelligence, he was constantly watched and interrogated. Oppenheimer, in charge of one of the nation's most secret wartime facilities, was never trusted completely.

In 1942 Oppenheimer was thirty-eight years old. A gifted teacher with a solid record of achievement behind him, he was credited with establishing at Cal Tech and Berkeley the greatest school of theoretical physics in the United States. Since 1941 he had been in charge of important research for the bomb project. Yet when Groves sought a director to head the centralized bomb production laboratory he envisioned, Oppenheimer was not an obvious choice. Though widely respected as a scientist, Oppenheimer was a security risk—from a military intelligence point of view—because of his Communist Party connections, however indirect they might seem. Most critically, he had none of the large-scale administrative experience believed necessary to head a program of such size and importance.

Nevertheless, if not the obvious choice, Oppenheimer was the man for the job as far as Groves was concerned. Not only was he impressed with what he called Oppenheimer's "genius," he believed there was no other qualified candidate available. Groves had his way. Against all objections from Army Intelligence, he rammed Oppenheimer's appointment through the Military Policy Committee in typical Groves style. The two men, so different in temperament, experience, and appearance, began a solid working relationship. A famous photo (see page 3 of photo insert) of the two taken in 1945 illustrates their physical disparity. Oppenheimer, dapper in suit, tie, and fedora hat, looks birdlike and fragile next to the robust General Groves, a bulky mass in wrinkled uniform.

Oppenheimer's work over the next several years was good for the Manhattan Project and good for him personally. He found in the Project a sense of duty and dedication to a cause he believed important. His organizational skills, humor, and understanding of people were much admired by those he supervised. According to colleague Victor Weisskopf,

> He did not direct from the head office. He was intellectually and even physically present at each significant step. . . . [H]is main influence came from his continuous and intense presence, which produced a sense of direct participation in all of us. It created that unique atmosphere of enthusiasm and challenge that pervaded the place. . . . It was most impressive to see Oppie handle that mixture of international prima donnas, engineers, and army officers, forging them into an enthusiastically productive crowd.[4]

Laura Fermi, wife of physicist Enrico Fermi and a resident at Los Alamos, also attributed most of the success of the bomb program to Oppenheimer, whom she called "the soul of the project."[5]

In the winter and spring of 1942–1943, Los Alamos took shape as a complex of laboratory, administrative, and residential buildings that became home and workplace to hundreds of scientists and their families for the next several years. The bomb work was concentrated in the Technical Area, including T-Building, which housed Oppenheimer's staff and the Theoretical Physics Division; the chemistry and physics building; assorted lab shops; a cryogenics lab; and a cyclotron building. Outside the main lab area, separated from it by high barbed-wire fences, was the community that supported the lab. It too was fenced for security. The fences bothered both American and European scientists who came to Los Alamos. For some of the latter, barbed wire was reminiscent of the concentration camps in their homelands.

Living conditions on the mesa (known only to the family and friends of residents as P.O. Box 1663, Santa Fe, New Mexico) were basic. Home for most was the cheaply constructed, army green, barracks-style, wooden building characteristic of military housing during the war. Families lived in apartment blocks, singles lived in dorms. All were heated (overheated, many complained) by coal-fired furnaces. Nearby, offering a contrast to the new and severely efficient military constructions, were the old buildings of the former boys' school, some built of hand-hewn logs, which served as additional living and dining facilities. The effect was unusual. Physicist Stanislaw Ulam's wife, Françoise, noted that "There was a feeling of mountain resort, in addition to army camp."[6]

While Los Alamos was being readied for its occupants, Oppenheimer began to scour the country for equipment and staff. The project's priority status and generous funding greatly aided the search for equipment, much of it borrowed from university laboratories. Getting a staff together proved more difficult and called into play Oppenheimer's powers of persuasion and the strength of his reputation in the scientific community.

Bringing key scientists to Los Alamos often meant

stealing them away from other important war work, like the radar project at the Massachusetts Institute of Technology (MIT). Oppenheimer had to make a strong case to Groves and Bush for each top scientist he wanted for the Manhattan Project. Then he had to sell the Project to the scientists, who would be required to lay aside current projects and move their families from comfortable surroundings to the Spartan environment of Los Alamos. In most cases, Oppenheimer got his people. He believed, and he could make others believe, that a successful atomic bomb project would shorten the war and save lives. Still, some had reservations about going to Los Alamos.

One particular issue, intellectual freedom, threatened to cripple Oppenheimer's recruiting efforts. For many scientists, working in an environment that permitted the flexible and free exchange of ideas and information was both the most successful way to practice science and central to the tradition of scientific inquiry. The progress of atomic physics since the turn of the century had been greatly aided by the free flow of information, both within nations and across national boundaries.

The sharing of ideas among scientists, through professional publications, international meetings, or informal "bull sessions," could and often did lead to significant new ideas and the recognition of important relationships that individuals in isolation might never have discovered. Scientists were proud of their membership in the international scientific community and opposed to the kind of regimentation and control of information that governments usually imposed in time of war. Hans Bethe, who came to Los Alamos to head the Theoretical Physics Division, believed he could not work effectively if stringent security regulations kept him away from his colleagues at the other Manhattan Project sites around the country. [7] Other Los Alamos scientists expressed similar thoughts.

Such views put them at odds with the military, and especially with General Groves, who was entrusted with the overall security of the Manhattan Project. This conflict over the issue of how and to what extent the work of scientists was to be managed by the military would continue throughout the life of the Manhattan Project and beyond.

Aside from the success of the Project, Groves's greatest concern and headache was security. Atomic secrets had to be protected from both the declared enemy and America's wartime ally, the communist government of the Soviet Union, which Groves considered to be a greater threat in the long run than either Germany or Japan. President Roosevelt had ordered the Manhattan Project to proceed with the utmost speed and security. Groves intended to follow those orders diligently, despite resistance from scientists who chafed under the army's security measures.

It had been Groves's original intention to achieve the tightest possible security for the bomb project by turning the Los Alamos laboratory into a military installation. Commissioned as military officers, project scientists would then be subject to military discipline and security regulations. But Oppenheimer knew his fellow scientists and understood that such conditions of employment would prevent recruitment of the best people. He and Groves worked out a compromise that split the administration of Los Alamos into civilian and military responsibilities. The University of California, under contract with the War Department, supervised the scientific and engineering work of the lab. No scientist was required to accept a commission. Oppenheimer, as site director, held responsibility for security within the laboratory compound. The army controlled the overall administration and security of the installation. This compromise did not satisfy everyone, but many scientists, though still wary of the government's intentions, accepted the compromise and joined the Los Alamos staff. Physicist Robert F. Bacher, appointed to head the project's Experimental Physics Division, threatened to resign if Los Alamos ever became a military installation (which it did not).

The scientists who worked on the atomic bomb often complained about the security arrangements and the effects these had on their work and home life. Their list of work-related irritants included: isolation from colleagues; the inability to share information with family members or even with fellow-scientists working on other aspects of the Project; and the invasion of privacy imposed by censored mail, telephone taps, and surveillance. Some fought back in small ways, such as writing letters in code or Chinese to challenge the censors. But in most cases they put up with the irritations in the interests of the war effort. Perhaps the attitude of Los Alamos scientists about security would have been different if they had learned sooner that one of their colleagues was a spy.

In an agreement worked out between British Prime Minister Winston Churchill and President Roosevelt at Quebec in August 1943, the Manhattan Project became a cooperative venture. The British Mission, which included emigré scientists from Austria, Germany, Poland, and Switzerland, arrived in Los Alamos in December to contribute its efforts to atomic bomb development. One of these trusted scientists, theoretical physicist Klaus Fuchs, was a spy who had been passing military secrets to the Soviet Union for a year. Highly placed in America's most sensitive military program, he would continue to steal and pass secret information until his discovery and capture in 1949. The routine of living and working went on at Los Alamos without anyone suspecting the hidden side of this polite, quiet, and hardworking man.

Life at Los Alamos was much the same mixture of ups

and downs found anywhere else, but on the mesa it was quickened and intensified. Los Alamos was a pressure cooker. The pressure grew out of the mission: to produce a workable and practical atomic bomb in the shortest possible time. Time, not money, was the most important concern: to get a bomb to shorten the war and to get it before anyone else.

The stress of the work, the effects of the mesa's high altitude, the inevitable personality conflicts among people who could not escape one another, the security regulations, the niggling inconveniences, all made life difficult at Los Alamos. Yet people coped. There were diversions. A community theater group blossomed. Oppenheimer himself appeared as a blood-drained corpse in the last act of *Arsenic and Old Lace.* People played late-night poker, square danced, went horseback riding, hiked, fished, and played baseball. Saturday night was for "whoopie," recalls Los Alamos resident Bernice Brode, remembering parties "both big and brassy and small and cheerful"[8] which helped to dissipate the hardness of life on the mesa. There was also a modest population explosion to which Robert and Kitty Oppenheimer contributed with the birth of a daughter on the third anniversary of Pearl Harbor, December 7, 1944. Despite the minimal living conditions, the shortages, the crowding, the personal grievances, there was a great camaraderie. A sense of cooperation and friendship, and the mutual dedication to something important, pervaded life at Los Alamos. The quality of Oppenheimer's leadership, his ability to organize and inspire, are often cited to help explain the Los Alamos spirit.

As the laboratory at Los Alamos took shape in the spring of 1943, Oppenheimer and his staff established their bomb-building priorities. The immediate tasks were to determine the best materials for a fission bomb, assemble a critical mass, and find a way to put it all together in an explosive package. All other work was subordinated to the solution of these problems. Also set aside was the development that had begun for an advanced generation of nuclear weapons—hydrogen bombs.

In 1941, Edward Teller had started thinking seriously about employing the fusion process to create a superbomb of immense power. Unlike nuclear *fission*—the splitting apart of the atomic nucleus—nuclear *fusion* releases energy through the joining together of small atomic nuclei to form larger ones, in the same kind of thermonuclear reaction that takes place in the sun.

From a military point of view, the "super," as it came to be called, had significant advantages over its fission counterpart. Its great explosive potential offered more power at less cost, more bang for the buck, as experts would say later. But, for the decision makers of the Manhattan Project, the hydrogen bomb had one major drawback. It needed an ordinary fission bomb as a trigger, and such a device did not yet exist. For the duration of the war, work on the super at Los Alamos would be restricted to theoretical studies only, and the fission bomb would remain the focus of the Manhattan Project.

In their early work on atomic bomb design, Los Alamos scientists and ordnance experts pinned their hopes on a gun-type bomb mechanism which would smash fissionable materials together to create a critical and explosive mass. In the favored plan, a U-235 or plutonium "bullet" would be shot into a "target" of similar material to form a critical mass. This mass, exposed to a neutron source crushed by the bullet, would begin to fission and release explosive energy.

The first gun bomb design, initially called "The Gadget" and then "Thin Man," was essentially a bomb welded to the mouth of a standard military cannon. As originally planned, Thin Man would measure about 2 feet (.6 m) in diameter by 17 feet (5.2 m) long and weigh in excess of 10,000 pounds (4,536 kg). Though a dummy Thin Man was eventually test-dropped by the army, refinements of design suggested by Italian emigré physicist Emilio Segrè in the fall of 1943 led to the creation of a bomb of more manageable size, nicknamed "Little Boy."

Little Boy, the bomb destined for Hiroshima, was about 6 feet (1.8 m) in length and weighed close to 9,000 pounds (4,082 kg). Scientists and weapons experts were so confident about the performance of Little Boy's gun mechanism that the bomb was never tested in an atomic explosion prior to its actual wartime use.

The gun bomb was a satisfactory design when U-235 was used to fuel the explosion. But, as scientists were distressed to find out, the gun device worked much too slowly for the fission of plutonium. This led to the development of a second, and faster, fission-inducing process called implosion. The implosion bomb, first proposed seriously by experimental physicist Seth Neddermeyer, used forces directed inward toward a center to create a supercritical (explosive) mass. As Neddermeyer first imagined it, the bomb would be a series of nested spheres: first a hollow core of plutonium, then a layer of natural uranium, and finally an outer sphere of high explosives. The detonation of the explosive layer would squeeze the uranium and the plutonium until the latter was reduced to a fissionable mass (see diagram in photo insert).

While the idea of an implosion bomb was straightforward enough on the blackboard, it offered tremendous problems to the scientists and engineers who tried to make it work. When Neddermeyer proposed the idea, his colleagues were skeptical. Creating the outer core of explosives and managing the forces it would release when detonated were the biggest problems of the implosion design. Energy would have to be uniformly transferred to

The first atomic bomb exploded before dawn broke on July 16, 1945. The mushroom cloud climbed 42,000 feet (12,800 m) into the overcast New Mexico sky.

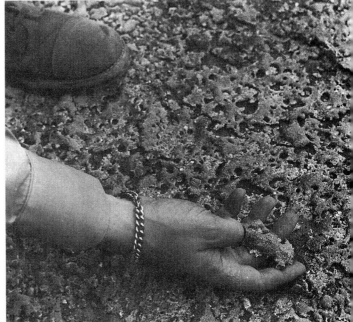

(Above) The Trinity blast dug this shallow crater 300 feet (91 m) around the tower from which the first atomic bomb hung. The steel tower was just about entirely disintegrated. (Right) Intense heat seared the sand around the tower into jade green, glasslike particles.

General Leslie Groves (right) and Dr. J. Robert
Oppenheimer stand next to the base of
the tower on which the bomb, Fat Man, hung.

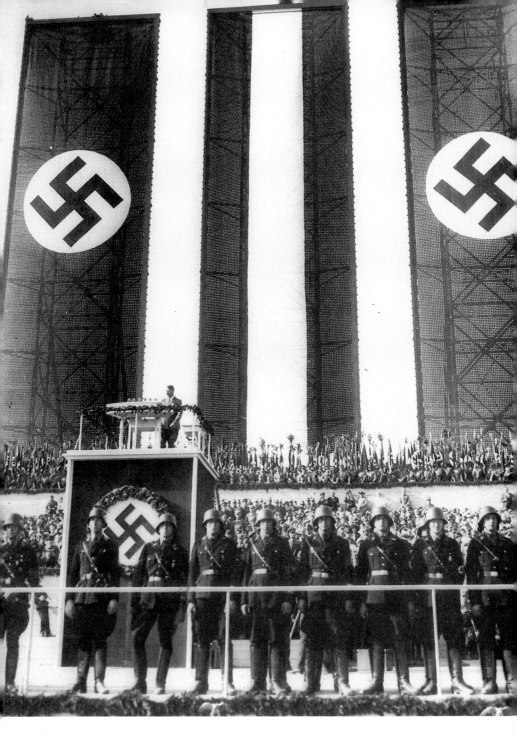

*The German menace: Nazi swastikas tower over
the platform from which Adolf Hitler addressed
a crowd of two million people.*

(Above) George L. Harrison (extreme left), consultant to Secretary of War Henry Stimson, flanks the three men who managed the Manhattan Project (left to right): General Leslie Groves, Dr. James Conant, and Dr. Vannevar Bush. (Left) Dr. J. Robert Oppenheimer, a professor of mathematical physics, served as wartime director of the Los Alamos laboratories where the first atomic bomb was developed and produced. One colleague called him the "soul" of the Manhattan Project.

(Above) Physicists Niels Bohr (left) and Max Planck. (Right) Enrico Fermi inspects equipment in his laboratory at Columbia University.

Brilliant minds that worked on the atomic bomb (clockwise, from top left): Albert Einstein, Edward Teller, Ernest Rutherford, Hans A. Bethe, and Lize Meitner

Klaus Fuchs, a nuclear scientist convicted of divulging the West's atomic bomb secrets to the Russians, served nine years in prison.

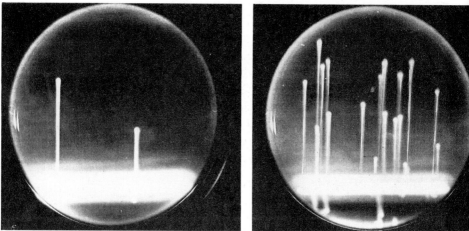

These two photographs capture stages during an atom-smashing experiment with uranium as the target. Each shaft in the "atomic thermometer" represents the amount of energy released by a smashed atom. As more atoms give up their energy, more shafts appear. Uranium shows the greatest burst of energy of any natural element.

This new cyclotron shown under construction at the University of Chicago boasts a magnet core that can accelerate protons to 450 million electron volts.

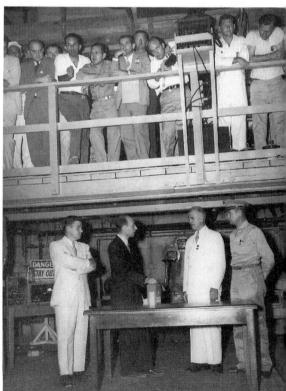

(Above) The sprawling plant at Hanford, Washington, produced plutonium fuel. (Right) Theoretical physicist Eugene Wigner (in dark suit) designed the plutonium-producing nuclear reactors in Hanford. He is shown here at the plant in Oak Ridge, Tennessee, which produced U-235 bomb fuel used for the atomic bomb that was dropped over Hiroshima.

(Left) Japan's surprise attack
on Pearl Harbor led
President Franklin Roosevelt
to sign the declaration
of war against Japan.

Churchill, Truman, and Stalin pose for
photographers during the Tripartite conference at
Potsdam, where the "Big Three" called for the unconditional surrender of all Japanese armed forces.

The B-29 Enola Gay *bomber* (below) *served as
the courier of death for thousands of Hiroshima
residents. The bomb shown above is similar to the
Little Boy type that detonated over the city.*

The Hiroshima blast in 1945 caused untold suffering for the Japanese. (Right) Tadako Enori suffered serious eye damage and could not blink or sleep with her eyes closed until she received surgical treatment in 1952.

This bomb resembled the Fat Man type of nuclear weapon that exploded over Nagasaki.

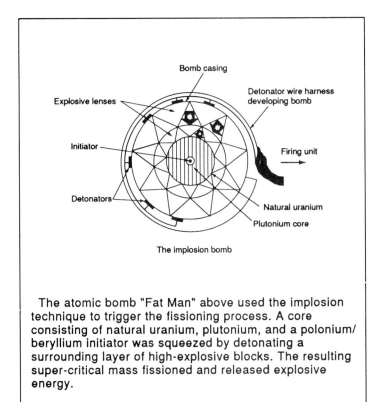

Bomb casing

Explosive lenses

Detonator wire harness developing bomb

Initiator

Firing unit

Detonators

Natural uranium

Plutonium core

The implosion bomb

The atomic bomb "Fat Man" above used the implosion technique to trigger the fissioning process. A core consisting of natural uranium, plutonium, and a polonium/beryllium initiator was squeezed by detonating a surrounding layer of high-explosive blocks. The resulting super-critical mass fissioned and released explosive energy.

Fat Man exploded over Nagasaki with a force equal to 22,000 tons of TNT. During the terrible aftermath, a salvager (left) sifts through the rubble.

(Top) Namoro Shigomitso signs on behalf of the emperor of Japan and the Japanese government during the formal rites of surrender held aboard the USS Missouri battleship in Tokyo Bay, August 31, 1945. (Bottom) American veterans and civilians celebrate Japan's surrender and the end of World War II.

the heart of the sphere in order to squeeze the plutonium center to a critical mass. This was a bit like squeezing water in your cupped hands without letting any squirt through your fingers, only much more difficult.

Neddermeyer and his team shattered the quiet of the Los Alamos mesa with frequent explosions as they experimented and practiced with implosive forces by using ordinary pipe, trying to squeeze the hollow pipe into a solid bar. Others joined the work on implosion. George Kistiakowsky, a Harvard chemist and explosives expert who came as a visiting consultant in the fall of 1943, joined the permanent staff in January 1944 and eventually took over supervision of the explosives research from Neddermeyer. The British scientists working at Los Alamos made important contributions to the implosion work. One of them, James L. Tuck, provided a breakthrough in design with the suggestion that the outer covering of explosives should be laid out in the form of closely fitting sections, which he called lenses, that would be fired by individual, precision-coordinated detonators. Eating up tons of high explosives each week, testing continued.

The technical problems were enormous. The explosive lenses, more than a hundred pieces altogether, had to be cast and machined to precise specifications calling for tolerances of a few thousandths of an inch. Multiple detonators had to be rigged to fire simultaneously. Scientists worked under great pressure. Not until mid-December 1944 were they able to achieve significant results with the implosion design. The deadline, a workable bomb by the time fissionable materials were ready in sufficient quantities, was approaching fast. In early 1945, special armed couriers escorted the first small quantities of precious U-235 bomb fuel on its cross-country train journey from the production site at Oak Ridge, Tennessee, to the desert laboratories of Los Alamos.

FUEL FOR A BOMB

While work to perfect the mechanism of the atomic bomb went on in the desert country of New Mexico, sites in Tennessee and Washington state produced the fissionable fuel that was the source of its destructive energy. As at Los Alamos, time was the major concern. Fear of German progress toward a bomb drove the fuel projects at a dizzying pace.

When Leslie Groves became officer in charge of the Manhattan Project in September 1942, he moved quickly to purchase 92 square miles (238 sq. km) of Appalachian scrub and hills near Knoxville, Tennessee, for a plant to produce U-235. The factory complex he built along the Clinch River was officially called the Clinton Engineer Works. Soon, people just knew it as Oak Ridge.

In the winter and spring of 1942–1943, workers transformed this chunk of Tennessee semiwilderness into a seven-gated, fenced reservation with more than 300 miles (483 km) of paved roads and streets, a rail network, and a new town—Oak Ridge—planned as home for 13,000 people. By late summer 1943, 20,000 construction workers had converged at the site to work on the hundreds of buildings that would house the huge machines and great power plants that would work around the clock to produce a daily quota of tiny lumps of U-235 to fuel the atomic bomb.

The difficult task of the scientists, engineers, and workers of the Oak Ridge complex was to separate two isotopes of uranium, U-235 and U-238, that were bound together in the natural form of the metal. Researchers discovered that only the former, the fissionable U-235, would serve as bomb fuel (see diagram page 52).

In the early stages of production, two processes—electromagnetic and gas diffusion separation—were employed to isolate U-235. The first had been demonstrated successfully by physicist Ernest O. Lawrence at Berkeley in 1941 and was more advanced when construction began at Oak Ridge. Lawrence's method was based on the principle that electrically charged atoms moving through a magnetic field traveled along the arc of a circle; the lighter the atom, the tighter the circle. Lawrence ionized uranium and subjected it to the magnetic field inside a converted cyclotron (a machine he invented for the high-speed acceleration of atoms), to achieve the separation of the light U-235 atoms from the heavier, and much more numerous, atoms of U-238. Because it worked atom by atom, the separation process was extremely slow. Eventually, after long-term operation, the modified cyclotron, renamed Calutron, would collect small quantities of pure U-235 in the form of minute flakes of metal.

At Oak Ridge the big Calutrons, called "racetracks" because of their oval shape, incorporated huge pumps and monster electromagnets. The latter were wound with hundreds of millions of dollars worth of wire made from silver borrowed from the U.S. Mint, silver that the punctilious General Groves carefully accounted for ounce by ounce. [1] At the height of production, almost 5,000 men and women worked around the clock under tight security and secrecy. They operated Calutrons in a process they did not understand for a purpose that could not be explained to them. The defense workers knew only that their long hours of labor were important to the war effort.

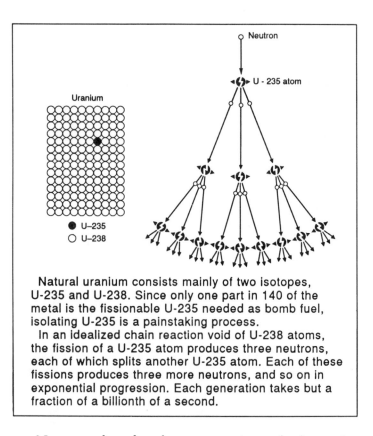

Natural uranium consists mainly of two isotopes, U-235 and U-238. Since only one part in 140 of the metal is the fissionable U-235 needed as bomb fuel, isolating U-235 is a painstaking process.

In an idealized chain reaction void of U-238 atoms, the fission of a U-235 atom produces three neutrons, each of which splits another U-235 atom. Each of these fissions produces three more neutrons, and so on in exponential progression. Each generation takes but a fraction of a billionth of a second.

Not sure that the electromagnetic method was the fastest or most efficient way to produce U-235, the government installed a second separation process at Oak Ridge. Gaseous barrier diffusion involved converting uranium to a gas, then using a superfine screen to isolate the lighter U-235 from the heavier U-238. The quantity of U-235 which could be isolated in a single gas diffusion tank was very small and the process extremely slow. Many successive screen separations were required to achieve the higher level of enrichment (an increase in the proportion of U-235 to U-238) necessary to make bomb-grade material. The gaseous barrier diffusion facilities of the Clinton Engineer Works, designated K-25, incorporated thousands of diffusion tanks on acres of floor space, some 2,000,000 square feet (186,000 sq. m) of production area.

Design problems and slow rates of production for both separation processes convinced Groves and Oppenheimer to install a third technology, thermal diffusion, at Oak Ridge. Philip Abelson, a Berkeley physicist working at the Naval Research Lab, developed thermal diffusion separation of U-235 independently of the Manhattan Project. Though Abelson was not supposed to know about the nation's highly secret bomb research, he had guessed enough to appreciate the importance of his own work to the progress of the Manhattan Project. He notified Oppenheimer through unofficial channels, and Oppenheimer passed the word to Groves.

Like the other separation methods, thermal diffusion took advantage of the different isotope weights. A vertical tank with hot and cold zones was filled with uranium hexafloride, a liquid. Lighter U-235 atoms migrated toward the hotter area of the tank; heavier U-238 atoms moved toward the colder region. The enriched material could then be siphoned off and passed to another tank to repeat the enrichment process.

Eventually the three separation technologies—electromagnetic, gas diffusion, thermal diffusion—were linked together to produce bomb-grade fuels in the·shortest time. In one such combination, scientists fed uranium enriched by thermal diffusion into Lawrence's Calutrons, thus greatly improving the rate of U-235 separation. By January 1945, Oak Ridge was producing 7.2 ounces (206 g or about the weight of a good-sized apple) of bomb-grade uranium daily and shipping it to Los Alamos.

Meanwhile, several thousand miles away in Washington state, another gigantic factory complex, the Hanford Engineer Works, was producing a second atomic fuel, plutonium, for the implosion bomb. Groves chose the Hanford, Washington site because it was isolated from

population centers—an important safety precaution—
and had readily available sources of power and the vast
amounts of water needed to cool huge chain-reacting
piles. The government purchased the land, 780 square
miles (2000 sq. km) around the tiny village of Hanford on
the Columbia River, near the end of January 1943. Soon
tens of thousands of construction workers—more than
40,000 by June 1944—swarmed over the site to build
roads, a town, three huge piles for plutonium production,
and three plants to separate plutonium from uranium.
Thousands more flocked to the site to live and work. In
just a year, the tiny village of Hanford blossomed into the
fourth largest city in Washington.

The piles that produced plutonium at Hanford were
larger versions of Fermi's successful CP-1 pile at Chicago
and a scale model, designated X-10, that had been
built and run successfully at Oak Ridge. Their construction and operation were beyond the capabilities of the
prime Manhattan Project contractor, Stone and Webster,
and were subcontracted to the firm of E.I. du Pont de
Nemours (Du Pont, for short) which had extensive experience in chemicals and explosives. Du Pont built the reactors, as the piles soon came to be called, to the designs of
theoretical physicist Eugene Wigner.

Wigner's reactor was a 28- by 36-foot (8.5 × 11 m)
graphite cylinder holding thousands of aluminum tubes
containing uranium slugs, each about the size of a roll of
quarters. The reactor's neutrons bombarded the slugs for
about 100 days, transforming one uranium atom in 4,000
to plutonium. Hot with radiation, the slugs were pushed
out the rear of the reactor by new slugs inserted at the
front. A deep pool of water held the slugs until short-term
radiation reached a manageable level. Some sixty days
later they went to the chemical separation site about 10
miles (16 km) away.

Problems with the first pile developed soon after it

began to operate on September 26, 1944. A fission by-product, xenon, was poisoning the reactor, causing the chain reaction to die. The problem was solved by installing more aluminum tubes to increase reactivity and neutralize the effects of the xenon. Plutonium production began in earnest in December 1944.

Plutonium can be separated from uranium by chemical methods, a far easier process than the complex isotope separation used at Oak Ridge. Hanford employed the separation chemistry developed by Glenn Seaborg at Berkeley and perfected at the University of Chicago, but on a much greater scale. Workers had to be protected from the hazards of dangerously radioactive substances produced in the reactors. Using remote control, they manipulated materials inside huge concrete structures for all but the final stages of the separation process. The final yields of the mighty production facilities of the Hanford Engineer Works were small quantities of purified plutonium nitrate which were shipped to Los Alamos by army ambulance. As the two powerful bomb fuels—U-235 and plutonium—began accumulating at Los Alamos in 1945, scientists made plans for the final preparation of the atomic bombs, Little Boy and Fat Man.

So high was the level of confidence in the reliability of Little Boy's gun mechanism, scientists decided that a full-scale test of the weapon was unnecessary. In April 1945 Otto Frisch of the British team fashioned a near-critical assembly of U-235 and determined the critical mass needed for a successful bomb. Little Boy was ready. The bomb was partially assembled into two sections. In July these were shipped separately, by water and air, to the Pacific island of Tinian for final assembly.

Scientists were less secure about the reliability and performance of the implosion bomb, Fat Man. A full-scale test was scheduled for July 15, 1945. Oppenheimer, for reasons never clearly explained, named the test Trinity.

5

DIFFICULT DECISIONS

The man whose decisions created the Manhattan Project, Franklin Delano Roosevelt, never lived to see the success of the Trinity test in July 1945. Three months earlier, on April 12, Roosevelt died of a massive stroke while sitting for his portrait. America was stunned. So was Vice President Harry S Truman, former senator from Missouri, who became the thirty-third president of the United States.

Truman inherited the responsibilities of a world leader and the hopes of a war-weary nation without the benefit of much experience in foreign affairs and diplomacy. He had not been close to Roosevelt and came to the office of president virtually ignorant of his predecessor's plans and methods. It was not a job he wanted, he explained to reporters on his first full day in office.

> *"Boys," I said, "if you ever pray, pray for me now. I don't know whether you fellows ever had a load of hay fall on you, but when they told me yesterday what had happened, I felt like the moon, the stars, and all the planets had fallen on me. I've got the most terribly responsible job a man ever had."* [1]

About one of his new responsibilities, the Manhattan Project and its development of the atomic bomb, President Harry S Truman knew almost nothing.

It was typical of Roosevelt's leadership style to exclude others from policy decisions, even those who ought to have taken part. As the Manhattan Project developed, he readily accepted the counsel of his science and military advisors—Bush, Conant, and Groves—on technical and administrative concerns. Political policy making, however, was a different matter. Roosevelt's thoughts went beyond the use of the atomic bomb as a weapon of war. He saw it also as a powerful tool of diplomacy which could be used to influence postwar relationships among nations, both former enemies as well as uncooperative allies such as the USSR, whose territorial ambition in eastern Europe was under growing suspicion. Roosevelt saw policy making as his personal responsibility and domain. As he grew to understand how the bomb might affect the postwar world, he reserved the right to make policy without consulting the people around him. This independence led to some major surprises for White House advisors concerned with the current and future use of atomic power. One such surprise grew out of the issue of Anglo-American cooperation for the development and control of atomic energy.

As early as 1940, even before the United States came into the war, Great Britain proposed the exchange of secret information on a variety of weapons projects. The early cooperation served American interests well. Not only had American and British scientists worked together well in the successful development of radar (the radio detection and ranging system used for defense), but the British MAUD Committee's report on the practical possibilities of building atomic weapons had helped to push ahead bomb research in the United States.

In 1941 Roosevelt approached British Prime Minister

Winston Churchill to suggest even closer scientific ties and a joint effort in the race for the bomb. The British welcomed this opportunity and their eventual contributions to the construction of the first successful atomic bomb were substantial. However, as the bomb program moved from development to production, some Americans began to have second thoughts about the wisdom of continued cooperation.

James Conant lobbied the president to discontinue the joint enterprise on the grounds that it was mainly a U.S. effort. Secretary of War Henry Stimson agreed with Conant and said that America was "doing nine-tenths of the work."[2] The question of Anglo-American cooperation centered around two postwar issues: who would control atomic weapons and who would benefit from the money-making potential of atomic power. Conant and Stimson felt so strongly about maintaining control of the emerging atomic energy industry that they were willing to risk losing British and Canadian support in the Manhattan Project, even if it meant waiting longer for a workable bomb. Though advised to discontinue the Anglo-American joint effort, Roosevelt did the exact opposite: he reaffirmed it. Furthermore, he kept some of the key details of this decision a secret from his own advisors.

On August 19, 1943, Roosevelt met Winston Churchill in Quebec, Canada, and signed a secret pact to continue cooperation on the bomb project. Churchill worked hard to get the agreement, though its terms placed Great Britain in the role of a lesser partner. Like Roosevelt, he saw the bomb not only as a means to end the war but also as a powerful bargaining chip in postwar international relations. It offered a means to maintain British strength in European affairs and contain the Soviet appetite for influence and domination. Roosevelt was sympathetic to Churchill's ambitions for Great Britain and believed a strong British presence in Europe would serve the best interests of the United States.

The Quebec Agreement included stipulations that: (1) the two countries would not use atomic bombs against one another; (2) mutual consent of the partners was required to use bombs against third parties; (3) information on making bombs would not be disseminated without mutual consent; and (4) the United States had sole commercial rights to the technology of atomic energy that grew out of joint research.

Churchill went home pleased at the deal he had cut. Roosevelt returned to Washington with a deal his atomic energy advisors did not learn about until after the president's death. Though an atomic bomb did not exist in 1943, it was a ghostly presence that nevertheless influenced thinking about the future. And scientists as well as political decision makers were concerned about the form that future would take.

Niels Bohr, who like Einstein enjoyed worldwide recognition as a scientist, came to the United States with the British team in 1943 to work as a consultant for the Manhattan Project. Bohr had recently used his prestige to convince the neutral government of Sweden to offer asylum to thousands of Jews in Nazi-occupied Denmark. Himself escaping to Sweden by boat, he was flown secretly to Great Britain in an unarmed Royal Air Force bomber with instructions to parachute into the North Sea should the plane be attacked. Bohr came to the United States under top secret cover, using the assumed name of Nicholas Baker. His colleagues at Los Alamos dubbed him "Uncle Nick." Had the Germans known of his arrival, Bohr's reputation as a theoretical physicist would have led them to guess the existence of the atomic bomb program. Yet "Uncle Nick" accepted involvement in the Manhattan Project not so much to work on the bomb as to work on the people who were making it. His personal mission was to convince American and British leaders that they must plan carefully for the responsible use of atomic energy after the war. Like Einstein, Bohr was an internationalist whose global point of view went beyond the interests of single nations. He saw clearly that atomic secrets would not remain secret for long. When other nations acquired the bomb, as Bohr was sure they would, the result would be a dangerous arms race for larger and more destructive weapons. "Unless," he wrote, ". . . some agreement about the control of the use of the new active materials can be obtained in due time, any temporary advantage, however great, may be outweighed by a perpetual menace to human security."[3]

Since the nuclear genie was already out of the bottle, Bohr argued, the Soviet Union must be made a partner in establishing international controls for atomic weapons. This should happen immediately, he concluded, before the bomb was actually constructed. He was confident that once governments understood the new reality created by atomic weapons—that war would mean mutual destruction—they would see that cooperation was in their best interest. Yet Niels Bohr, for all his vision, good sense, and faith in people to make rational decisions, was mistaken in his assumptions. Those in power listened to his message but did not accept it.

Because of his stature as a Nobel Prize winner and scientific leader, Bohr was allowed to present his case in person to both Churchill and Roosevelt. The interview with the British prime minister was a disaster. "We did not speak the same language," Bohr later recalled.[4] Churchill not only rejected outright the idea of international control and cooperation with the Soviet Union, he questioned Bohr's competence to deal with political concerns. In Churchill's mind, the atomic bomb was just another bomb after all and did not change the principles of warfare or statecraft. If new problems should arise, then he and FDR would work them out. Churchill envisioned a world in which Great Britain and America successfully held an atomic monopoly, what former President Theodore Roosevelt would have called "a big stick," to keep unreasonable nations in line. And since the Soviet Union was clearly one of the "unreasonable nations," sharing vital military secrets with the likes of communist dictator Joseph Stalin was clearly out of the question.

While FDR seemed to be more sympathetic to Bohr's ideas of international responsibility and control, he supported Churchill's position in the end. Bohr was bitterly disappointed. Eventually the prejudice against international supervision of atomic energy, especially as it involved the Soviets, was carried into the early Truman administration where, if anything, it hardened as disagreements with the Soviet Union increased.

By the time Harry Truman became president of the United States, the war in Europe was winding down. On D-Day, June 6, 1944, Allied forces under Supreme Commander Dwight D. Eisenhower had landed at Normandy and gained the foothold in Europe that signaled the beginning of the end for Germany. Over the next 11 months as Allied armies pushed German forces from the west, the Russians shoved from the east. A desperate Nazi counteroffensive launched in December was effectively checked at the Battle of the Bulge. On April 30, as the victors were entering Berlin, Adolf Hitler committed suicide. Germany surrendered unconditionally on May 7, 1945. The war in Europe, which had eaten up the lives of nearly 39 million people, was over.

America now turned its full attention to the war in the Pacific. The atomic bomb, originated as a weapon to be used against Germany, was now being readied for possible use on Japan.

Following their successful attack on Pearl Harbor,

Japanese forces had swept through Southeast Asia and the Pacific with relative ease to capture Indochina, Burma, Malaya, Singapore, the Dutch East Indies, and the Philippines. It was not until June 1942 at the Battle of Midway Island in the central Pacific that the war began to go badly for the Japanese. By 1945 they were fighting a defensive war. Allied forces recaptured the Philippines and took Okinawa, a site for air bases within striking distance of the Japanese home islands. Fighting turned ferocious as the Allies pressed their advantage. The typical Japanese soldier was willing to sacrifice and endure the most horrible privations to preserve honor—his own and that of the emperor. He willingly died before suffering the shame of surrender or capture. This tenacious and fanatic resistance resulted in heavy American casualties. Beautiful and exotic Pacific islands were turned into killing fields.

At Iwo Jima, eight square miles of volcanic island in the western Pacific, American marines died by the thousands trying to root out an enemy who fought to the death. Iwo Jima was one of many such engagements on islands of rock, coral, and jungle whose names few Americans had ever heard of before. The fighting was sickening, demoralizing, and often incomprehensible. What could be done with people who died with such reckless abandon, who had to be burned out of caves with flamethrowers and explosives, who flew their planes into American ships in hundreds of kamikaze (suicide) raids?

The performance of Japanese soldiers and airmen convinced many Americans that Japanese civilians on the home islands would resist invasion with the same ethic of sacrifice. What this might cost in terms of American casualties was of deep concern to the American leaders who were faced with using the atomic bomb. One military estimate said that 1,000,000 American soldiers would be killed or wounded in an invasion of Japan. It seemed to be a question of them or us.

Truman learned of the atomic bomb on his first day in office. After the president's first press conference, Secretary of War Henry Stimson asked to see him "about a most urgent matter."

> Stimson told me that he wanted me to know about an immense project that was under way—a project looking to the development of a new explosive of almost unbelievable destructive power. That was all he felt free to say at the time, and his statement left me puzzled. It was the first bit of information that had come to me about the atomic bomb, but he gave me no details. [5]

Two weeks later Stimson briefed him more fully on the entire Manhattan Project and the importance of the bomb for the war and beyond. Mindful of the future, Stimson urged the president to form a committee to consider the potential problems America might face in the nuclear age. Truman agreed and created the Interim Committee on S-1, headed by Stimson, to study and report on wartime and postwar applications of atomic energy. A scientific panel consisting of Oppenheimer, Lawrence, Arthur Compton, and Fermi was formed to advise the larger group on science-related matters.

The Interim Committee met on May 31, 1945, and took its job seriously. In his opening statement as chairman, Secretary of War Stimson spoke of the "new relationship of man to the universe" which the development and use of atomic energy had brought about and pointed out that this new force "must be controlled if possible to make it an assurance of future peace rather than a menace to civilization."[6] The committee then went on to recommend the use of the atomic bomb against Japan as soon as possible and without warning. In reaching their decision, the members of the committee claimed the atomic bomb as a legitimate weapon of war that could and should be used to encourage Japanese surrender. They were convinced that the public would want the bomb used quickly to prevent further loss of American lives, especially since so much of the nation's effort and resources had been expended to build it. The committee considered, then ruled out, a demonstration of the bomb outside Japan. Such a demonstration risked failure (an embarrassment), and would give advance warning which could jeopardize any subsequent effort to drop the bomb on Japan. The committee's science panel, headed by Oppenheimer, concurred with the findings of the larger group. It saw no value in a technical demonstration of the bomb's power and "no acceptable alternative to direct military use."[7]

Though the Interim Committee report reflected the majority point of view among top scientists and decision makers connected with the Manhattan Project, not everyone agreed. A panel of scientists from the Met Lab in Chicago issued the Franck Report (named for its chairman, James Franck) which criticized a surprise use of the atomic bomb on political grounds. The report argued that "the use of nuclear bombs for an early unannounced attack against Japan [was] inadvisable." Not only would such "indiscriminate destruction" cause the United States to lose the support of world opinion and lead to an arms race, it would jeopardize the possibility of ever reaching agreement on the international control of nuclear weapons.[8] The Interim Committee reviewed the scientists' concerns expressed in the Franck Report but stuck to its original recommendation for a surprise attack against Japan. Only one of the eight members dissented, and then not immediately.

In a surprise move three weeks after the Interim Committee report was issued, committee member and Navy representative Ralph A. Bard withdrew his support of the recommendation on humanitarian grounds. In a War Department memorandum, Bard wrote that "before the bomb is actually used . . . Japan should have some preliminary warning." He based his opinion on the "position of the United States as a great humanitarian nation" and on the "fair play attitude" of the American people.[9] Shortly after, and for the same reason, Bard resigned his post as under secretary of the Navy. On this issue of surprise use of the bomb, Bard was not supported by other members of the Interim Committee. Yet many of the scientists who had helped to build the bomb also protested its unannounced use against Japan on moral grounds.

A petition circulated by Leo Szilard offered the opinion that a nuclear weapon should be used against Japan only if that country clearly understood the threat it faced and still refused to surrender. In a letter to Oppenheimer, Szilard maintained that it was important for dissenting scientists to exercise "their right given to them by the Constitution to petition the President."[10] The petition, dated July 17, 1945, and signed by sixty-eight Manhattan Project scientists, was concerned with the moral issue and said that any military advantages achieved by the surprise use of the atomic bomb against Japan would be canceled by the horrified reaction of world opinion to the immorality of such an action. The president, if indeed he ever saw the petition, was not swayed.

President Truman probably made the decision to use the bomb on Japan without warning soon after reviewing the Interim Committee's recommendation, but he seems to have always assumed that it would be used. "The final decision of where and when to use the atomic bomb was up to me," Truman says in his memoirs. "I regarded the bomb as a military weapon and never had any doubt that it should be used."[11] He began to anticipate the success of the first bomb test as he made preparations for a summit conference with Churchill and Stalin at Potsdam, Germany. The president even suggested July 15, 1945 for the meeting, a date picked to coincide with the test of Fat Man at Alamogordo, New Mexico.

Truman, a longtime poker player, understood the advantage of having an "ace in the hole" for his first across-the-table negotiations with Stalin. Potsdam was an important diplomatic test for the inexperienced president who, while used to the rough and tumble of domestic politics, was unsure of himself in an international setting. The agenda included: the strategy to end the war in the Pacific; the question of Soviet involvement in that war; the future of Germany; and the issue of Soviet authority in Europe, a matter much on the president's mind. The Russians were being troublesome and Truman felt he must stand firm. The atomic bomb, the president's "ace in the hole," would give him the position of strength he needed to deal effectively with the communists.

The attitude of the American government toward Joseph Stalin and the Soviet government had been hardening since the early days of the Truman presidency. In an effort to create a buffer zone of states around their borders, the Soviets installed sympathetic governments in the Eastern European countries they liberated from German occupation. Particularly loathsome to Americans was the use of the Soviet organized secret police (OGPU) and control of the press to manipulate political events in ways favorable to Moscow. Hungary was seen as the victim of this kind of heavy-handed maneuvering, and American leaders at the time of the Potsdam Conference feared that Poland was to become the next Soviet puppet. Truman was determined to resist continued Soviet expansion.

Thus the Potsdam Conference began in an atmosphere of distrust which never dissipated, and relations between the Soviet Union and her western Allies continued to sour. As attitudes hardened, Truman placed more and more faith in the bomb as a moderator of Soviet attitudes and actions.

As the Big Three assembled in Potsdam, scientists assembled the test bomb in New Mexico. The original schedule called for the explosive test of Fat Man, the implosion bomb, on July 14, 1945. In the face of some problems with final preparation, Oppenheimer requested a three-day delay. Groves denied the request on the grounds that Truman needed positive results for Potsdam. In any case, the explosion did not occur until July 16. A preliminary report of the successful test reached Truman at Potsdam the same day, and Groves's full report followed a few days later.

Truman got his "ace in the hole." He was elated, and the news infused his participation at the conference with a new vigor and confidence noted by both Churchill and Stalin. With the bomb in his pocket, Truman felt America no longer needed Soviet help to end the Pacific war, help for which the Soviets might well demand territorial concessions.

At Potsdam, the president informed Stalin that America possessed a "new weapon of unusual destructive force." Stalin "showed no special interest," Truman recalled, but said that he was "glad to hear it and hoped we would make 'good use of it against the Japanese.' "[12] The almost casual response hid the fact that Stalin already knew a great deal about the bomb through the efforts of Soviet spy Klaus Fuchs, who had infiltrated the Manhattan Project in 1943 through its team of British scientists.

The Potsdam Conference gave rise to the Potsdam Declaration, which offered the Japanese the opportunity to end the war by "the unconditional surrender of all

Japanese armed forces," or risk the alternative of "prompt and utter destruction."[13] The Japanese did not know they were being threatened by atomic bombs. Japanese Prime Minister Baron Kantaro Suzuki rejected the language of Potsdam and vowed to "resolutely fight for the successful conclusion of the war."[14] For many Japanese leaders, even those who were inclined favorably toward surrender, the term "unconditional surrender" was a hindrance. It implied a threat to abolish the institution of emperor, or worse, to try the emperor, thought to be a god by the Japanese, as a war criminal. Such actions were unacceptable to the Japanese, and American leaders did not try to dispel their fears. The war continued to grind on.

On July 24 the administration officially released the atomic bomb to the Air Force for use against Japan. Groves's orders, approved by Marshall and Stimson at Potsdam, authorized the 509th Composite Group based on Tinian Island to deliver Little Boy as soon after August 3 as weather permitted and Fat Man sometime after August 6 should Japan refuse to surrender. Additional bombs were to be used as they were readied.

6

THE FIRST NUCLEAR WAR

In June 1945 the first 509th combat crews landed on Tinian Island in their sleek silver B-29 Superfortresses. Construction workers had transformed the once sleepy island 6,000 miles (9,600 km) from the United States into the world's largest airport. Six runways, looking like so many superhighways, became the springboard for hundreds of planes making conventional air strikes in the Pacific. Now Tinian began to gear up for a single strike which would be the biggest of them all.

Group commander of the 509th, Lt. Col. Paul W. Tibbets, trained the crews for the secret atomic bomb mission which the military had code-named Silverplate. He would pilot the plane carrying Little Boy. The 225 officers and over 1,500 enlisted men selected for the group had been carefully winnowed and sieved by Tibbets from the Air Force's best. They flew the newest versions of the B-29 at cruising speeds of 220 mph (354 kmph) and altitudes in excess of 30,000 feet (9144 m), safe from anti-aircraft fire and beyond the reach of most fighter planes. For months Tibbets's men had practiced, at Wendover Field in Utah and again on Tinian Island, the special tactics developed to drop the bomb successfully and also survive the experience. They rehearsed sharp diving turns after releasing practice bombs, bright orange imitations of Fat Man nicknamed "Pumpkins." On August 5 the crews, the planes, and the bomb were ready.

On August 6, ordnance workers loaded Little Boy into the bomb bay of the B-29 which Tibbets had named *Enola Gay* after his mother. A crew member described the bomb as "an elongated trash can with fins."[1] At takeoff time the bomb was complete except for the insertion of the cordite explosives into the breech of the gun mechanism. Cordite would fire the U-235 bullet into its uranium target to achieve critical mass. At 2:45 A.M., in the warm dark of a South Pacific morning on Tinian, an overloaded *Enola Gay* used up all of her runway to rise noisily into the air and head for Japan.

Little Boy's target was Hiroshima, one of four cities (along with Kokura, Niigata, and Nagasaki) chosen as potential targets. Each had a military installation and none had been attacked by conventional bombing. Though these targets were selected for the maximum psychological impact their destruction would have on the Japanese, a fifth city was ruled out for the same reason. Secretary of War Stimson argued that Kyoto, the former ancient capital and intellectual center, with its hundreds of temples, was a national cultural treasure, the loss of which would embitter the Japanese and strengthen their resolve against surrender. His personal intervention saved Kyoto from the horror that would soon engulf Hiroshima.

As the *Enola Gay* flew toward Hiroshima, weapons officer Captain Deke Parsons inserted the cordite explosives and finally, at 7:30 A.M., armed the bomb. A sophisticated three-stage firing system ensured that the bomb would explode at the desired altitude. There was nothing left to do but drop it. The B-29 and two accompanying observation planes flew over Hiroshima unchallenged. Many citizens of the city looked up to watch the big bombers—"B-sans" they called them—high in the air. Since harmless observation flights over the city were not unusual, few headed for cover. The bombardier took over control of the plane from Tibbets and maneuvered to his aiming point, the Aioi bridge in central Hiroshima.

The uranium bomb, Little Boy, exploded at 8:16 A.M. Hiroshima time with a force equivalent to between 12,000 and 15,000 tons of TNT. In one giant burst of energy, World War II became the world's first nuclear war. Hiroshima was turned into a living laboratory for the study of nuclear destruction.

When Little Boy detonated at 1,900 feet (580 m) above a hospital, the resulting fireball contained million-degree temperatures. Heat energy radiated from the bomb in two closely spaced bursts, which flashed over the city at light speed. The thermal blasts inflicted burns of all degrees of seriousness, even, as frequently observed at Hiroshima, causing human skin to peel off in large sheets. Several miles away from the explosion's center, many of the people who happened to be looking at the *Enola Gay* when the bomb exploded were blinded by the sun-hot flash.

Near the area of ground zero most objects, including buildings and people, just disappeared, vaporized by the heat. A bit further away people were reduced to small charred lumps on roads and sidewalks. Fires burst out all over the city. That day's conditions of temperature, wind, and availability of fuel created an enormous firestorm which sucked away large volumes of air from the burning city and killed thousands by asphyxiation. This also happened earlier at Tokyo under conventional bombing. Many of those who survived the terrible heat of Little Boy did not escape the effects of air blast.

When the bomb exploded, its energy pushed a wave of air away from ground zero at slightly faster than the speed of sound. The wave created excessive air pressure (over-pressure) which spawned high winds that knocked down buildings, people, and almost everything else for several miles. Many thousands of people were killed or wounded by falling buildings or from the effects of high-velocity rubbish—broken glass, wood splinters, bricks, and all the other bits and pieces a city is reduced to by an atomic bomb. Some were themselves turned into missiles that struck solid objects with great force and came apart. Eye-witnesses described tripping over heads and seeing people without arms or feet, though still alive, covered with blood from the effects of flying debris. At Hiroshima the worst of the air blast damage occurred within a radius of 3 miles (5 km) from ground zero. Glass windowpanes were broken as far as 12 miles (20 km) away.

In his 1946 book *Hiroshima*, John Hersey tells the stories of six Hiroshima residents who experienced and survived the blast. One of them, Mrs. Hatsuyo Nakamura, was in her house when Little Boy exploded high over the city.

> As Mrs. Nakamura stood watching her neighbor, everything flashed whiter than any white she had ever seen. She did not notice what happened to the man next door; the reflex of a mother set her in motion toward her children. She had taken a single step (the house was 1,350 yards, or three-quarters of a mile, from the center of the explosion) when something picked her up and she seemed to fly into the next room over the raised sleeping platform, pursued by parts of her house.
>
> Timbers fell around her as she landed, and a shower of tiles pommelled her; everything became dark, for she was buried. The debris did not cover her deeply. She rose up and freed herself. She heard a child

cry, "Mother, help me!," and saw her youngest—
Myeko, the five-year-old—buried up to her breast and
unable to move. As Mrs. Nakamura started fran-
tically to claw her way toward the baby, she could see
or hear nothing of her other children. [2]

Mr. Kiyoshi Tanimoto, a Methodist minister who was in the suburbs when the explosion occurred, made his way into the city to check on his family and church. He met the wounded moving in the opposite direction.

[H]e met hundreds and hundreds who were fleeing,
and every one of them seemed to be hurt in some way.
The eyebrows of some were burned off and skin hung
from their faces and hands. Others, because of pain,
held their arms up as if carrying something in both
hands. Some were vomiting as they walked. Many
were naked or in shreds of clothing. On some un-
dressed bodies, the burns had made patterns—of un-
dershirt straps and suspenders and, on the skin of
some women (since white repelled the heat from the
bomb and dark clothes absorbed it and conducted it to
the skin), the shapes of flowers they had had on their
kimonos. Many, although injured themselves, sup-
ported relatives who were worse off. Almost all had
their heads bowed, looking straight ahead, were silent,
and showed no expression whatever. [3]

The devastation of the exploding atomic bomb severely crippled the city's ability to care for its people. It not only wounded many thousands of people, but also destroyed the medical facilities and killed the doctors and nurses needed to care for these wounded. Those, like Dr. Terufumi Sasaka, who were still able to provide medical help were soon overwhelmed.

By nightfall, ten thousand victims of the explosion had invaded the Red Cross Hospital, and Dr. Sasaka, worn out, was moving aimlessly and dully up and down the stinking corridors with wads of bandage and bottles of mercurochrome, still wearing the glasses he had taken from the wounded nurse, binding up the worst cuts as he came to them. Other doctors were putting compresses of saline solution on the worst burns. That was all they could do. After dark, they worked by the light of the city's fires and by candles the ten remaining nurses held for them. Dr. Sasaka had not looked outside the hospital all day; the scene inside was so terrible and so compelling that it had not occurred to him to ask any questions about what had happened beyond the windows and doors. Ceilings and partitions had fallen; plaster, dust, blood, and vomit were everywhere. Patients were dying by the hundreds, but there was nobody to carry away the corpses. Some of the hospital staff distributed biscuits and rice balls, but the charnel-house smell was so strong that few were hungry. By three o'clock the next morning, after nineteen straight hours of his gruesome work, Dr. Sasaka was incapable of dressing another wound. 4

A less visible carrier of death than heat and air blast was the lethal radiation (gamma rays) released by the atomic bomb. It caused radiation sickness in thousands of people close to ground zero. Radiation sickness is a hopeless disease, usually resulting in death. In the first few days following the explosion, thousands died of radiation poisoning. Many others lingered on in great pain for weeks before they died, suffering the effects of radiation sickness—vomiting, diarrhea, bleeding, anemia, hair loss, and vulnerability to infection. Hospitals that survived the blast were full of such patients. Some victims recovered slowly and lived on for years, then died of leukemia and other cancers associated with excessive radiation exposure.* Survivors also suffered the mental anguish of having lived through the terror of a nuclear explosion, the hell on earth which destroyed family, friends, and the normalcy of their lives in a huge ball of fire.

Little Boy killed over 100,000 people outright, wounded another 100,000 and destroyed about 90 percent of the city of Hiroshima. One bomb easily consumed the whole tightly woven fabric of a city of 400,000 people. Yet while the first atomic bomb was a roaring success as a weapon of war, it opened to mixed historical reviews.

Hearing the news of the Hiroshima explosion during his return trip from Potsdam, President Truman called it "the greatest thing in history."[5] Soon, opinion polls would show that a majority of Americans supported the use of the atomic bomb and the president's reasons for using it. Yet not everyone agreed. Representing a minority point of view, Leo Szilard described the Hiroshima attack as "one of the greatest blunders in history . . . from the point of view of our moral position."[6] Shortly after Hiroshima, another bomb was ready for delivery.

President Truman, through General Groves, authorized the Air Force to drop the second atomic bomb (Fat Man) as soon after the first as final preparations and weather permitted. Originally scheduled for August 11,

---

*The health of persons exposed to high radiation in Hiroshima was followed in great detail for many years. More than 1,000 persons died of cancer, presumably due to nuclear radiation.

There was no fallout in the Hiroshima bombing because the bomb was released at high altitude. One finding of the careful investigation was that there was no noticeable genetic effect in the children of the people exposed to radiation.

the attack was moved ahead to August 9, only three days after Hiroshima. The interval gave the Japanese little time to learn about and evaluate fragmented reports from the devastated city. Truman issued another demand for unconditional surrender, warning of more Hiroshimas to come. Radio broadcasts and leaflets dropped on major cities encouraged the Japanese to ask about events in Hiroshima and petition the emperor to end the war. But the speed of events and continued resistance by the Japanese military leadership to surrender condemned another city to die.

In early morning, August 9, *Bock's Car*, a B-29 piloted by Major Charles W. Sweeney, rose from Tinian with Fat Man in its belly and flew toward the prime target, Kokura. Bad weather over the city forced a switch to the alternate target, the port city of Nagasaki. Soon after 11:00 A.M., at a height of 1,650 feet (500 m), Fat Man exploded with a force of 22,000 tons of TNT. Because of the placement of the bomb and surrounding hills which contained the explosion, the devastation was less widespread than at Hiroshima. But the horror was the same. Nagasaki burned for twenty-four hours. Initially some 40,000 people were killed and another 25,000 injured.

More bombs were being readied, but President Truman gave orders to halt the attacks, saying he didn't like the killing of "all those kids."[7] More bombs proved unnecessary. In the face of die-hard military opposition at home, Emperor Hirohito forced the issue of surrender and accepted the terms of the Potsdam Declaration. "I cannot bear to see my innocent people suffer any longer," he said. "Ending the war is the only way to restore world peace and to relieve the nation from the terrible distress with which it is burdened. . . . The time has come when we must bear the unbearable."[8] The war was over.

Americans celebrated August 14 as Victory Over

Japan Day (VJ-Day). Church bells rang, jubilant crowds danced in the streets, fireworks filled the skies, and war-weary citizens from New York to San Francisco greeted the peace with a flourish of uncorked energy. As Americans celebrated, the Japanese grieved for a nation defeated in war and for two cities sacrificed for the cause of peace.

EPILOGUE
THE LEGACY OF THE
MANHATTAN PROJECT

Very few things have happened in the history of the United States, or of the world for that matter, that have had the impact of the Manhattan Project. That first atomic blast at Alamogordo, and the second and third in Japan, set into motion a chain of events that changed the course of human affairs by influencing domestic and international politics, the world economy, and the ways that people think about themselves and the future. In many cases the pace of change has outdistanced the human ability to cope with it.

With its display of atomic muscle at Hiroshima and Nagasaki, the United States showed itself to be the world's strongest military power. Though the nation's entire atomic arsenal consisted of only a few bombs, more could easily be produced. What this newfound capability would mean for the future had been the subject of considerable speculation and discussion among the select number of people privy to atomic secrets. Despite this concern, the United States entered the atomic age with few actual plans. "Wait and see" was the approach to the future, at least in the early postwar period.

The months following the end of the war were a time of uncertainty and confusion for the atomic bomb development program. Making a bomb to help end the war had been the mission of the Manhattan Project. Since that mission had been achieved, what would happen at the Project facilities—Los Alamos, Hanford, and Oak Ridge—in the future? No one had ready answers.

The men and women of Los Alamos, tired of wartime pressures and restrictive living conditions on the mesa, were anxious to return to a more normal life and get on with the peace. Many project scientists went back to the research and teaching they had left for war work. Hans Bethe returned to Cornell University. Leo Szilard moved his career away from physics and into biology. J. Robert Oppenheimer, about to be vaulted into the public spotlight for his role in the atomic bomb program, left to assume the directorship of the prestigious Institute for Advanced Study at Princeton. A few key scientists chose to stay on. Teller would have stayed, given support for his special interest, the hydrogen bomb. However, sensing a lack of enthusiasm for such work, Teller joined the faculty of the University of Chicago instead.

Oppenheimer was replaced as director at Los Alamos by Norris Bradbury, who had organized the assembly of the bomb for the Trinity test. Bradbury headed Los Alamos during a difficult time, when control and funding of the atomic energy program were shifting from the military to the hands of Congress. It was a slow transition made difficult by a lack of firm direction from the Truman administration and conflicting ideas about the future of atomic weapons. Those who favored building more bombs saw the bombs as a way to ensure future peace; those against believed they were far too dangerous to have around for any reason.

Some of the Manhattan Project scientists would have been pleased to see the bomb program end. Two days after the Japanese surrender, the scientific panel of the S-1

Interim Committee (Oppenheimer, Lawrence, Compton, and Fermi) discussed the future of atomic weapons in a letter to the administration. The panel members perceived in that future a world threatened by weapons of even greater destructive power than currently existed. Against these weapons, the scientists said, there would be no adequate defense. They urged the need for political change because "the safety of this nation . . . cannot lie wholly or even primarily in its scientific or technical prowess. It can be based only on making future wars impossible."[1] In short, the panel saw no good reason to continue development of the atom bomb. However, the idea of abandoning the bomb, which the United States had worked so hard to create at a cost of billions of dollars, was not popular with policy makers in Washington. The atomic bomb program continued to move forward, though it bumped along haltingly.

By 1946 more specific planning and thinking about the future of atomic energy became evident. Congress created the Atomic Energy Commission (AEC) to control and regulate the development of the U.S. atomic energy program. The AEC appointed a General Advisory Committee, headed by Oppenheimer, to offer scientific and administrative expertise for the commission's deliberations.

Then, in the postwar flush of enthusiasm for the work of the United Nations, the Truman administration led an effort that brought into being a world authority, the United Nations International Atomic Energy Commission, to control the peaceful uses of atomic energy. The United States representative to this body, Bernard M. Baruch, made a bold and innovative proposal for control of nuclear weapons production. The Baruch Plan aimed to ensure the peaceful use of atomic energy through the international supervision of atomic reactors and their products. Further, the United States promised to destroy all of its atomic bombs when inspection procedures designed to prevent future manufacture were in place throughout the world.

The Soviet Union rejected the Baruch Plan, the first of many such disagreements over arms control that became a feature of cold war relations among the superpowers. The Soviets feared that the Baruch Plan would reduce their sovereignty and may have doubted the sincerity of the American proposal. While calling for the abolition of nuclear weapons, the Truman administration proposed to continue their testing, a policy which both nations followed thereafter. Also the Russians had their own bomb program and wanted to neutralize the American advantage in weaponry, a possibility taken seriously only by American scientists.

Disdainful of Soviet scientific abilities, American military and political leaders expressed confidence that the USSR would not produce an atomic weapon easily or soon. President Truman was of this number and seemed to believe that only Americans had the "know-how" to achieve such technological development. When asked by a reporter if the United States might sometime share its nuclear secrets with other nations, Truman replied, "Well, I don't think it would do any good to let them in on the know-how, because I don't think they could do it anyhow."[2] General Leslie Groves expressed a similar attitude. Author Merle Miller remembers a speech given by Groves in 1945 in the Grand Ballroom of New York's Waldorf-Astoria Hotel.

The general stood a little away from where the fillet of beef had been, and he said, the words loud and clear, that the United States didn't need to worry about the Russians ever making a bomb. "Why," he said, smiling, "those people can't even make a jeep."[3]

Soon, however, the president, General Groves, and other skeptics were proven wrong.

Sometime between August 26 and 29, 1949, at a site in Siberia, the Soviet Union exploded its first atomic bomb, nicknamed Joe I by the U.S. press corps, after Joseph Stalin. Americans were shocked, especially those who took comfort in the supposed backwardness of Soviet technology. The U.S. response to the Soviet success was to inject new life and large amounts of money into its own weapons program. The big bang of Joe I was the starting gun for the next round of the arms race, which would rapidly turn into a long distance competition.

The General Advisory Committee of the AEC met in response to news of the successful Soviet test. It recommended development of more atomic weapons using current modes of technology but specifically rejected a high priority for work on the Super, or hydrogen, bomb. The H-bomb was a weapon of mass destruction only, said the Oppenheimer-led committee, and would not improve the security of the country. Soon administration advisors and government scientists were taking sides for and against H-bomb development. Truman listened to the debate, then decided to accelerate the hydrogen bomb development program. The laboratories at Los Alamos were busy once again and Edward Teller was back in the bomb business.

On November 2, 1952, the world's first hydrogen bomb, code-named Mike, vaporized Elugelab Island in the South Pacific with a force equivalent to 10.4 megatons (one megaton = one million tons) of TNT. Exploding with the power of 1,000 Hiroshima-sized bombs, Mike catapulted the arms race onto a new and higher level of human destructive potential, and at a bargain price. Relatively cheap to produce compared with early bombs, Supers became the superpowers' weapon of choice. The

Soviet Union, not to be outdone in the quest for parity as a nuclear power, tested more atomic bombs and then its own full-fledged H-bomb in 1955. And so, the same deadly game of "catch up and get ahead" continued, a race with no apparent finish line except the Big Finish.

Fear of the enemy produced the bomb and that same fear fueled the arms race. Frequent hostilities short of war between the United States and the Soviet Union have become a fact of life since the last years of World War II. The columnist Walter Lippmann coined the term "cold war" to describe this poisonous atmosphere of East-West tension. Many times the temperature of the cold war was raised to dangerous levels by world events: Communist insurgency in Greece and Turkey in the late 1940s; a Soviet backed coup in Czechoslovakia; the blockade of West Berlin in 1948; the Korean War of the 1950s; the downing of a U.S. spy plane in the Soviet Union; the Cuban missile crisis of 1962; Afghanistan.

Some cold war confrontations ended in mere posturing and sword-rattling threats, as when President Truman sent a fleet of "nuclear capable" B-29s to England during the Soviet blockade of Berlin in 1948. In other cases the world has been led to the brink of war. President John F. Kennedy and Soviet Premier Nikita S. Khrushchev brought their nations very close to a nuclear shoot-out over the issue of Russian missiles in Cuba. "[T]wo scorpions in a bottle," was the way Robert Oppenheimer put it, "each capable of killing the other, but only at the risk of its own life."[4]

Whole generations of Americans were born and grew up in the hostile atmosphere of the cold war. Russia was perceived as the enemy, working to spread communism throughout the world and destroy democracy. "We will bury you," Soviet Premier Nikita Khrushchev said to America.[5] A series of celebrated spy trials and investigations in the early 1950s helped to instill the fear of communism which became a part of the American character.

In 1949, British agents arrested Klaus Fuchs, Manhattan Project scientist, for passing both American and British atomic secrets to the Soviets for seven years. Fuchs was convicted the following year and sentenced to prison. Soon thereafter, the U.S. government apprehended Julius and Ethel Rosenberg, Communist party members, on charges of espionage. The Rosenbergs became the first American civilians to be executed for passing atomic secrets. Then, when a State Department official, Alger Hiss, was arrested and accused of spying, apprehension grew about the infiltration of Communists into the American government. A junior senator from Wisconsin, Joseph McCarthy, turned these fears into a militant and nationwide anti-Communist crusade.

McCarthy's particular brand of witch-hunting, based on groundless accusations and suspicions, came to be called McCarthyism. Eventually discredited by his Senate colleagues, McCarthy fell into disgrace and out of the public limelight, but not before instilling the fear of communism and the Russians into many an American citizen. In 1954 Robert Oppenheimer, the man who led the nation's most top secret military project during the war, was caught in the anti-Communist net. Because of his early left-wing political leanings, "imprudent and dangerous associations" with known Communists, and "fundamental defects in his character,"[6] the Atomic Energy Commission stripped Oppenheimer of his security clearance and barred him from further participation in nuclear weapons development and policy. Though never formally charged with treason, or even disloyalty, Oppenheimer left government service under a cloud of suspicion created by a nation's fear of its enemy. That fear continued to grow as the Soviet Union made progress in developing its nuclear weapons arsenal.

As long as the United States held a nuclear monopoly the Soviet Union considered itself in an inferior negotiating position. When the Soviets achieved parity, the rules of the game changed. Both countries adopted a policy of mutual deterrence: try to use your weapons to destroy us, the superpowers threatened one another, and we will destroy you with ours. This policy of high-stakes nuclear tit-for-tat came to be called MAD, short for mutually assured destruction. In a world governed by MAD thinking, each side sought more and more destructive weapons to counter the improved weapons made by its enemies. With each opponent armed to the teeth, everyone was supposed to feel more secure since no one could possibly be crazy enough to start a war, an act of national suicide.

The harvest of this planting of distrust and hatred is a current world crop of more than 50,000 nuclear weapons, from 58-pound (26.3 kg) land mines with the power of 10 tons of TNT to multi-megaton missile warheads equivalent in explosive power to thousands of Hiroshima-type bombs. Many of the weapons, designed to be delivered by plane or missile (ground- and sea-launched), the United States and the Soviet Union have targeted at one another. Even the use of a modest number of these weapons would turn great chunks of warring nations into wasteland and destroy the rich economic, political, and social glue that holds a country together. And then there are the global consequences of nuclear war to think about, such as the effects of nuclear winter and environmental contamination. However, for their peace of mind and sanity, most people would rather not think about them at all. It is much easier to believe that nuclear war could never occur.

For the United States the cost of creating its vast collection of nuclear weapons and developing the means to deliver them has been astronomical. After World War II, Americans realized that their old isolationist ways were dangerous in the nuclear age and committed the country to a program of high level military readiness. This has led to the appearance of a more or less permanent war economy in peacetime, with a substantial portion of the nation's resources committed to military needs. The result of this quest for security has been a huge financial burden for tax-paying Americans and, some would argue, a diminished standard of living. Spokesmen for the government and the military-industrial complex it created have claimed that large military spending has been good for the nation because it put millions of people to work, thus sparing the country from the effects of large-scale unemployment. There is room for doubt.

Skeptical economists argue that the money would be better spent trying to put people to work in the private sector. Huge defense spending has actually eaten up the country's resources which otherwise might have been used to produce consumer goods and services, thereby raising everyone's standard of living. Nuclear weapons and missiles may or may not keep people safe, but they are not directly useful to consumers. They don't toast bread, plow fields, carry people to work, or educate children. Further, it is claimed, huge defense budgets totaling trillions of dollars since World War II have been paid for by deficit spending (when the government has to borrow money and keeps going deeper into debt), which contributes to inflation and shrinks the purchasing power of everyone's dollars. In addition, the emphasis on producing military hardware has gobbled up a significant portion of the investment capital needed to increase the productivity of American industry and make it competitive in world markets. A world leader in military spending, the United States of America is the world's number-one debtor nation. For many Americans this has become an important moral issue. Can the United States continue to expend scarce resource dollars and much of the nation's scientific talent on weapons of mass destruction or on expensive, and possibly unworkable, defense systems (like former president Ronald Reagan's proposed Strategic Defense Initiative, or "Star Wars") at the cost of neglecting the general well-being of its citizens?

The problems of security in a world bristling with "nukes" (as popular culture has nicknamed nuclear weapons) has been made more difficult by their spread to other nations. The nuclear club is small but growing. It has six declared members: the United States, the Soviet Union, Great Britain, France, China, and India. Two other countries, Israel and South Africa, won't admit to being club members but either have the weapons or could make them quickly. Iraq, Libya, Pakistan, and North Korea probably want to join the club and, it is feared, appear to be working toward that goal.

The facts are not pleasant to consider. The number of nuclear weapons continues to grow. More countries are getting them. Also weaponry is becoming so complicated and speedy that control over it is being taken out of human hands and shifted to computers. Small conflicts and conventional wars are all too numerous and any of these might lead to the use of nuclear weapons, especially in desperate situations. Terrorists are becoming bolder and more strident in their demands and might turn to nukes if they could buy or steal them. And then, of course, accidents do happen. In June 1980, the computer warning system at U.S. Air Force Strategic Air Command headquarters in Omaha, Nebraska, announced that the United States was under attack by Soviet missiles. In the confusion that followed, crews of over 100 American nuclear bombers, B-52s, were ordered to start the engines of their planes in case a quick takeoff was necessary. Soon it was determined that some malfunction of equipment had caused the faulty warning. The alert was called off. Within a few days of the incident, investigators discovered the problem: a tiny computer chip had failed.[7] This was not the first time such a malfunction took place; it is not likely to be the last. Computer hardware breaks down, software fails, people make mistakes. There are just too many possibilities for things to go wrong. Recognizing the dangers that exist, the nuclear powers have, on occasion, made efforts to limit them.

Talks between Soviet Premier Nikita Khrushchev and American President John F. Kennedy resulted in the first test-ban treaty (1963). To limit the contamination of nuclear fallout, the two countries agreed not to test weapons in the atmosphere, in space, or under water. Underground testing, however, was permitted and has continued, with a few pauses, up to the present. Other agreements since have attempted to limit the spread of nuclear weapons to other countries (non-proliferation agreements) and to limit the numbers of offensive and defensive weapons held by the U.S. and USSR. The latter grew out of negotiations in the 1970s called Strategic Arms Limitations Talks (SALT). A new round of negotiations known as Strategic Arms Reduction Talks (START) began in 1982 and continues today. Despite these efforts to make the world safer from the threat of nuclear weapons, the danger has continued to grow. People still feel insecure and threatened, and with good reason. They live in a world in which nations hostile to one another keep building weapons of mass destruction while still believing that war is a natural and inevitable activity of human beings. They have a right to be scared.

If the nations of the world put their collective wills to it, they could destroy all nuclear weapons in a very short time, and everyone could breathe a bit easier. For a while. What the world can never be rid of is the knowledge of how to build nuclear weapons. Such knowledge will continue to exist no matter how many well-intentioned treaties and agreements may be signed. Nations will make weapons if they really want to do so. Somehow people will have to learn to live with that fact.

From the earliest beginnings of the Manhattan Project the destructive potential of nuclear weapons has made people afraid for the world. Some have spoken out, both within the early circles of secrecy and in public as more information about nuclear power became known. Scientists such as Einstein, Bohr, Szilard, and Oppenheimer have expressed opposition to nuclear policy. Committees and commissions, world leaders representing opposing ideologies, religious leaders, and military leaders have all addressed the need to control and even abolish the new breed of weaponry. And the people have spoken out. From the early days of "Ban the Bomb" campaigns, to the large protest rallies of the 1960s, to militant resistance in the 1980s, Americans by the thousands have opposed the trend toward more and more destructive nuclear weapons. Some have demanded complete disarmament while others have promoted international agreements to "freeze" weapon development or cut back the numbers of weapons. Protesters have also expressed their growing concerns about environmental issues. These have included the contamination of areas surrounding nuclear weapons and materials production sites, the safe and responsible disposal of radioactive wastes, and the transportation of potentially dangerous nuclear weapons and fuels through areas of high population.

Despite the concerned and sometimes angry voices of protest raised against the government's policy of maintaining a powerful nuclear arsenal, many Americans have supported the arms buildup as regrettable but necessary in a dangerous world. Strength of nuclear arms, they argue, has prevented a nuclear war from occurring. The divisions caused by these differing points of view have created rifts in American society which still exist today. Yet despite all the talk and all the effort to make the world safer, either by eliminating or making more nuclear weapons, the fact remains that the world still lives in the terrible shadow of the mushroom cloud. Though we have understood the crux of the problem all along, we have not been able to do much about it.

"[T]he unleashed power of the atom," said Albert Einstein of the impact of nuclear weapons, "has changed everything save our modes of thinking, and we thus drift toward unparalleled catastrophes."[8] In 1945 a declaration of the United States, Great Britain, and Canada on the control of atomic energy stated that "the only complete protection for the civilized world from the destructive use of scientific knowledge lies in the prevention of war."[9] As long as people continue to operate under the old way of thinking that tolerates war as an acceptable, and perhaps even inevitable, way to settle the differences between nations, the world can never be free of the nuclear threat.

There may be no better time for change than now, the decade of the 1990s, as political revolutions sweep through Eastern European countries that have been called Soviet satellites for more than forty years. Surprising political events, different in shape and unfinished, jostle one another for attention on the front pages of the world's newspapers and lead news analysts to the question "Is the Cold War over?" The Berlin Wall, that powerful symbol of Cold War division and hostility, is down, and its rubble is hawked as souvenirs of a bygone era. The reunification of East and West Germany seems more a matter of when than if. Old-line Communist regimes in Poland, East Germany, Czechoslovakia, Romania, and Bulgaria have succumbed to popular demands for change and increased freedom.

Accompanying these changes and making them possible, have been parallel changes initiated in the Soviet Union in 1985 when Mikhail Gorbachev came to power. Under the banners of *perestroika* (reconstruction) and *glasnost* (openness), President Gorbachev has sought to restructure Soviet society and transform a sickly economy. The changes at home are dependent on better relations abroad. This has led to a more conciliatory Soviet policy toward the United States and a significant warming of the international political atmosphere. It is too soon to be sure about what these events will mean for the future. They may mean that the time is ripe for nations to escape the human, economic, and political burdens of the Cold War. A significant reduction in nuclear armaments would be a significant first step toward a safer, saner, and more peaceful world. But such a courageous act would require effort, trust, and a continuing commitment to the cause of peace.

We know what must be done. The Manhattan Project showed what creative and brilliant minds, a strong dedication to a cause, lots of united human energy, international cooperation, and the spending of vast quantities of money could accomplish in a relatively short time. What a new focus of such forces could do for the cause of lasting peace is a matter of conjecture. That it must be done is a matter of survival.

ACKNOWLEDGMENTS

PHOTOGRAPHY CREDITS

GLOSSARY

NOTES

BIBLIOGRAPHY

INDEX

ACKNOWLEDGMENTS

Thank you to all who helped in the writing of this book, particularly my wife, Georgette Frazer, and our friend and neighbor in Malaysia, Debra Blake Weisenthal.

—D. E. B.

The editors wish to thank Hans A. Bethe, professor emeritus of physics of Cornell University, for giving us the benefit of his expertise. His high standard of scholarship and his commitment to scientific and historical accuracy have greatly enriched this book.

PHOTOGRAPHY CREDITS

Photographs courtesy of: AP/Wide World Photos: pp. 1, 4, 5 bottom, 9, 10, 16 bottom; UPI/Bettmann Newsphotos: pp. 2, 3, 5 top, 6 bottom, 7 top and center left, 8, 11 bottom, 12 top, 13, 14, 15; American Institute of Physics: pp. 6 top (Niels Bohr Library/Margrethe Bohrs Collection), 7 top right (Niels Bohr Library/Hoover Institution), 7 center right, 7 bottom (both Meggers Gallery of Nobel Laureates); The Bettmann Archive: pp. 11 top, 12 bottom, 16 top.

GLOSSARY

ALSOS—The code name for the U.S. intelligence unit organized in 1943 to assess German progress toward constructing an atomic bomb and to capture German scientists, laboratory facilities, and raw materials. The word is Greek for "grove," a veiled reference to Brigadier General Leslie R. Groves, who organized the mission.

atom—The smallest particle of matter which cannot be divided by chemical means. Atoms are the building blocks of the universe.

atomic bomb—A nuclear weapon whose energy comes from the fission of heavy elements, such as uranium or plutonium. Also called the atom bomb or A-bomb.

Atomic Energy Commission (AEC)—The civilian agency created in 1946 to oversee the atomic energy program of the United States. Also the body of five persons, appointed by the president, to direct the agency.

Bock's Car—The name given to the B-29 Superfortress, which dropped the atomic bomb Fat Man on Nagasaki, Japan.

cadmium—A soft, silvery white metal, atomic number 48, with an atomic weight of approximately 112. Because it is an effective absorber of neutrons, cadmium is used to control the process of fission in nuclear reactors.

Calutron—A particle accelerator devised by Ernest Lawrence to separate the uranium isotopes U-235 and U-238.

chain reaction—A reaction that occurs when a nucleus absorbs a neutron and fissions, or splits, thereby releasing additional neutrons that are absorbed by still other nuclei to continue the fission process.

classical physics—The study of the properties of matter and energy prior to the development of the theory of relativity and quantum theory shortly after the turn of the twentieth century.

cordite—An explosive made from nitroglycerine and cellulose nitrate.

critical mass—The smallest quantity of fissionable material that will support a self-sustaining chain reaction.

cryogenics—The study of materials and phenomena at temperatures close to absolute zero.

cyclotron—A particle accelerator, invented by physicist Ernest Lawrence, in which charged particles are brought up to very high speeds by subjecting them to powerful electric and magnetic fields.

$E = mc^2$—Energy equals mass times the speed of light squared. Albert Einstein's equation, the basis of all nuclear energy, showed the possibility of releasing enormous amounts of energy in an atomic bomb.

electromagnetic separation—A method of separating isotopes which uses the fact that atoms of different atomic weights will separate from one another when forced to move at high speeds in a particle accelerator.

electron—A negatively charged elementary particle forming part of the atom. Electrons surround the positively charged nucleus and determine the chemical properties of the atom.

emigré—One who emigrates from or leaves a country, often for political reasons, to settle elsewhere.

Enola Gay—The nickname given to the B-29 Superfortress which dropped the atomic bomb Little Boy on Hiroshima, Japan.

fallout—Airborne particles containing radioactive material that fall to the ground following a nuclear explosion.

Fat Man—The nickname given to the implosion-type atomic bomb tested at Alamogordo, New Mexico, on July 16, 1945 and then dropped on Nagasaki, Japan, on August 9, with an estimated explosive force of 22,000 tons of TNT.

fission—See nuclear fission.

fusion—See nuclear fusion.

gas diffusion separation—A method of separating isotopes based on the fact that gas atoms with different weights will diffuse through a porous barrier (like a very fine screen) at different rates.

graphite—A very pure form of carbon, used along with natural uranium to construct the first nuclear pile (reactor) at the University of Chicago in 1941. In the pile, neutrons slowed down by graphite were more likely to continue the fission process.

ground zero—The point on the surface of land or water vertically below or above the center of the burst of a nuclear explosion.

hydrogen bomb—A nuclear weapon that derives its vast energy largely from fusion. The hydrogen bomb's thermonuclear reaction is triggered by a fission bomb. Also called H-bomb, thermonuclear bomb, fission-fusion bomb, or "super."

implosion—The process of compressing, or squeezing together, fissionable material in a bomb so that it becomes supercritical and produces a nuclear explosion.

ionize—The process of adding one or more electrons to, or removing one or more electrons from, atoms, thereby creating electrically charged atoms known as ions.

isolationism—A policy of attempting to keep one's country away from entangling international political and economic relations.

isotope—One of two or more atoms of the same element which are nearly identical in chemical behavior but differ in the number of neutrons each possesses.

Joe I—The first atomic bomb tested by the USSR. Exploded sometime between August 26 and 29, 1949, the bomb was named by the U.S. press after Soviet leader Joseph Stalin.

Little Boy—The nickname given to the gun-type, fission atomic bomb dropped on Hiroshima, Japan.

MAUD—The code name for the British committee formed in 1940 to review the potential for making an atomic bomb.

Mike—The code name for the first hydrogen bomb, tested by the United States in the South Pacific on November 2, 1952.

nuclear fission—The splitting of a heavy atomic nucleus into two approximately equal parts, accompanied by the release of large amounts of energy and one or more neutrons.

nuclear fusion—The fusing, or joining together, of lighter atomic nuclei to form a heavier nucleus, which releases large amounts of nuclear energy.

nuclear power—The energy produced by a nuclear reaction.

nuclear reactor—A device in which a nuclear fission chain reaction can be started, maintained, and controlled. It is the basic machine of nuclear energy.

Pax Atomica—Like the Pax Romana of the Roman Empire, a period of relative peace created and enforced by military power.

pile—The original term for a nuclear reactor, so used because the first reactor, built by Enrico Fermi at the University of Chicago in 1941, was constructed by piling up graphite blocks and natural uranium.

plutonium—A heavy, radioactive metallic element with atomic number 94 and atomic weight of 242. Plutonium is man-made in nuclear reactors. Its most important isotope is fissionable P-239, used to fuel the bomb tested at Alamogordo, New Mexico, on July 16, 1945.

proton—A positively charged elementary particle which is a part of the nucleus of all atoms.

quantum theory—The modern physical theory, growing out of the work of German physicist Max Planck, which is based on the idea that energy is not emitted or absorbed continuously but rather in units or quanta. Quantum theory and the theory of relativity together form the theoretical basis of modern physics.

radioactive—Exhibiting radioactivity, the spontaneous disintegration of an unstable atomic nucleus accompanied by the emission of energy in the form of alpha- or beta-particles and/or gamma rays.

reactivity—The measure of a nuclear reactor's neutron release.

subatomic particle—A part of an atom: electron, proton, neutron, etc.

supercritical mass—The quantity of fissionable material required to initiate a self-sustaining and uncontrollable nuclear chain reaction leading to an explosion.

Sword of Damocles—In classical Greek mythology, Dionysius gave a banquet at which a sword was suspended by a hair over the head of Damocles in order to show the precariousness of power.

thermal diffusion separation—One of the methods used at Oak Ridge, Tennessee, to separate the isotopes U-235 and U-238. In a tank filled with uranium hexafluoride, U-235 atoms moved toward the hotter area of the tank and U-238 atoms moved toward the colder.

thermodynamics—The branch of physics dealing with the nature of heat and its conversion into other forms of energy.

Thin Man—The nickname of an early version of Little Boy, the atomic bomb dropped on Hiroshima.

TNT—The chemical explosive trinitrotoluene. The power of nuclear explosions is expressed in terms of the weight of TNT which would release the same amount of energy when exploded.

uranium—A naturally occurring, radioactive element with the atomic number 92 and an atomic weight of approximately 238. Its isotope U-235 provided the fuel for the atomic bomb dropped on Hiroshima.

U-238—An isotope comprising 99.3 percent of natural uranium. U-238 is not fissionable and is not used as atomic bomb fuel.

U-235—An isotope comprising 0.7 percent of natural uranium. It was separated from U-238 at Oak Ridge, Tennessee, and provided the fuel for the atomic bomb dropped on Hiroshima.

Xenon—An inert gas, atomic number 54, with an approximate atomic weight of 131.

NOTES

Prologue: The Day Everything Changed

1. Quoted in Len Gionannitti and Fred Freed, *The Decision to Drop the Bomb* (New York: Coward-McCann, 1965), p. 197.
2. Mark Sommer, *Beyond the Bomb: Living Without Nuclear Weapons* (Chestnut Hill, Mass.: Expro Press, 1985), p. 149.
3. Ibid., p. 146.
4. Ibid., p. 150.

Chapter 1: The Road to Manhattan

1. Laura Fermi, *The Story of Atomic Energy* (New York: Random House, 1961), p. 69.
2. Spencer R. Weart and Gertrud Weiss Szilard, eds., *Leo Szilard: His Version of the Facts* (Cambridge, Mass.: MIT Press, 1978), p. 62.

Chapter 2: The Race for the Atomic Bomb

1. "Charles A. Lindbergh: America First" in *The Second World War and After: 1940–1949*, The Annals of America, Vol. 16 (Chicago: Encyclopaedia Britannica, 1976), p. 74.
2. "Albert Einstein: Letter to President Roosevelt" in *The Great Depression 1929–1939*, The Annals of America, Vol. 15 (Chicago: Encyclopaedia Britannica, 1976), p. 601.
3. Jack Dennis, ed., *The Nuclear Almanac: Confronting the Atom in War and Peace* (Reading, Mass.: Addison-Wesley, 1984), p. 22.
4. Ibid.
5. Martin J. Sherwin, *A World Destroyed: Hiroshima and the Origins of the Arms Race* (New York: Vintage Books, 1987), p. 29, 35–36.

6. Quoted in Richard Rhodes, *The Making of the Atomic Bomb* (New York: Simon and Schuster, 1986), p. 369.

Chapter 3: Blueprint for a Bomb

1. Quoted in Peter Wyden, *Day One: Before Hiroshima and After* (New York: Simon and Schuster, 1984), p. 67.
2. Quoted in Peter Goodchild, *J. Robert Oppenheimer: Shatterer of Worlds* (Boston: Houghton Mifflin, 1980), p. 56ff.
3. Victor F. Weisskopf, "The Los Alamos Years" in I.I. Rabi et al., *Oppenheimer* (New York: Charles Scribner's Sons, 1969), p. 26.
4. Ibid., p. 25.
5. Fermi, *The Story of Atomic Energy*, p. 133.
6. Quoted in Rhodes, *The Making of the Atomic Bomb*, p. 565.
7. Sherwin, *A World Destroyed*, p. 57.
8. Quoted in Rhodes, *The Making of the Atomic Bomb*, p. 565.

Chapter 4: Fuel for a Bomb

1. Rhodes, *The Making of the Atomic Bomb*, p. 490.

Chapter 5: Difficult Decisions

1. Harry S. Truman, *Year of Decisions* (Garden City, N.Y.: Doubleday, 1955), p. 19.
2. Quoted in Sherwin, *A World Destroyed*, p. 72.
3. Quoted in Wyden, *Day One*, p. 122.
4. Quoted in Rhodes, *The Making of the Atomic Bomb*, p. 530.
5. Truman, *Year of Decisions*, p. 10.
6. "Notes of the Interim Committee Meeting, May 31, 1945" in Sherwin, *A World Destroyed*, p. 296.
7. "Science Panel: Recommendations on the Immediate Use of Nuclear Weapons, June 16, 1945" in Sherwin, *A World Destroyed*, p. 305.
8. "The Franck Report (Excerpts from a Report to the Secretary of War, June 11, 1945)" in Dennis, *The Nuclear Almanac*, pp. 38–39.
9. Ralph Bard, "Memorandum on the Use of S-1 Bomb" in Sherwin, *A World Destroyed*, p. 307.
10. Quoted in Ibid., p. 217.
11. Truman, *Year of Decisions*, p. 419.
12. Ibid., p. 416.
13. "Proclamations by Heads of Governments, United States, United Kingdom, and China" in Ibid., p. 392.
14. Quoted in Rhodes, *The Making of the Atomic Bomb*, p. 693.

Chapter 6: The First Nuclear War

1. Quoted in Rhodes, *The Making of the Atomic Bomb*, p. 701.

2. John Hersey, *Hiroshima* (New York: Bantam Books, 1946), pp. 10–11.
3. Ibid., pp. 38–39.
4. Ibid., pp. 60–61.
5. Truman, *Year of Decisions*, p. 421.
6. Quoted in Rhodes, *The Making of the Atomic Bomb*, p. 735.
7. Ibid., p. 743.
8. Quoted in Wyden, *Day One*, p. 302.

Epilogue: The Legacy of the Manhattan Project

1. Quoted in Rhodes, *The Making of the Atomic Bomb*, pp. 751–752.
2. Quoted in Robert J. Donovan, *Tumultuous Years: The Presidency of Harry S. Truman 1949–1953* (New York: W.W. Norton, 1982), p. 102.
3. Merle Miller, *Plain Speaking: An Oral Biography of Harry S. Truman* (New York: Berkley Publishing Corp., 1973), p. 228ff.
4. "J. Robert Oppenheimer: Atomic Weapons and American Policy" in *Cold War in the Nuclear Age 1950–1960*, The Annals of America, Vol. 17 (Chicago: Encyclopaedia Britannica, 1976), p. 209.
5. Quoted in Julius W. Pratt, *A History of United States Foreign Policy*, 2d ed. (Englewood Cliffs, N. J.: Prentice-Hall, 1965), p. 470.
6. "The Oppenheimer Case" in *The Cold War in the Nuclear Age: 1950–1960*, The Annals of America, pp. 289–292.
7. Ground Zero, *Nuclear War: What's in It for You?* (New York: Pocket Books, 1982), pp. 242–243.
8. Quoted in Jonathan Schell, *The Fate of the Earth* (New York: Knopf, 1982), p. 188.
9. "The Control of Atomic Energy" in *The Second World War and After: 1940–1949*, The Annals of America, p. 341.

BIBLIOGRAPHY

The Annals of America. Vols. 15–18. Chicago: Encyclopaedia Britannica, 1976.

Bainbridge, Kenneth T. "A Foul and Awesome Display." *Bulletin of the Atomic Scientists*, May 1975:40–46.

Baird Joel, et al. *The Nuclear Arsenal Reader*. Cambridge, Mass.: Harvard Educators Concerned About Nuclear War, 1984.

Bard, Ralph A. "War Was Really Won Before We Used A-Bomb." *U.S. News and World Report*, August 15, 1960:73–75.

Bernstein, Barton J., and Allen J. Matusow, eds. *The Truman Administration: A Documentary History*. New York: Harper Colophon Books, 1966.

Bethe, Hans. "Comments on the History of the H-Bomb." *Los Alamos Science*, Fall 1982:43–53.

Brown, Anthony Cove, and Charles B. MacDonald, eds. *The Secret History of the Atomic Bomb*. New York: Delta, 1977.

Dennis, Jack, ed. *The Nuclear Almanac: Confronting the Atom in War and Peace*. Reading, Mass.: Addison-Wesley, 1984.

Donovan, Robert J. *Tumultuous Years: The Presidency of Harry S. Truman 1949–1953*. New York: W.W. Norton, 1982.

Feldbaum, Carl B., and Ronald J. Bee. *Looking the Tiger in the Eye: Confronting the Nuclear Threat*. New York: Harper and Row, 1988.

Fermi, Enrico. "The Development of the First Chain-Reacting Pile." *Proceedings of the American Philosophical Society*, Vol. 20, January 1946: 20–24.

Fermi, Laura. *Atoms in the Family*. University of Chicago Press, 1954.

Gannon, William, ed. *The Effects of the Atomic Bombs on Hiroshima and Nagasaki, by the United States Strategic Bombing Survey*. Santa Fe: Gannon, 1973.

Gionannitti, Len, and Fred Freed. *The Decision to Drop the Bomb*. New York: Coward-McCann, 1965.

Goodchild, Peter. *J. Robert Oppenheimer: Shatterer of Worlds*. Boston: Houghton Mifflin, 1980.

Groves, Leslie. *Now It Can Be Told*. New York: Harper and Row, 1962.

Hawkins, David. *Manhattan District History: Project Y, the Los Alamos Project*. Los Angeles: Tomash, 1983.

Heisenberg, Werner. "The Third Reich and the Atomic Bomb." *Bulletin of the Atomic Scientists*, June 1968: 34–35.

Hersey, John. *Hiroshima*. New York: Modern Library, 1946.

Hewitt, Paul G. *Conceptual Physics*. 5th ed. Boston: Little, Brown, 1985.

Hitler, Adolf. *Mein Kampf*. New York: Reynal, 1940.

Jette, Eleanor. *Inside Box 1163*. Los Alamos: Los Alamos Historical Society, 1977.

Kunetka, James W. *City of Fire: Los Alamos and the Atomic Age 1943–1945*. Albuquerque, N.M.: University of New Mexico Press, 1979.

Lifton, Robert Jay. *Death in Life: Survivors of Hiroshima*. New York: Random House, 1967.

Manhattan Engineer District (MED or Manhattan Project) files. National Archives, Washington, D.C.

Miller, Merle. *Plain Speaking: An Oral Biography of Harry S. Truman*. New York: Berkley, 1973.

Moore, Ruth. *Niels Bohr*. Cambridge, Mass.: MIT Press, 1985.

Office of Scientific Research and Development, Section 1 (OSRD, S-1) files. National Archives, Washington, D.C.

Pratt, Julius W. *A History of United States Foreign Policy*. Englewood Cliffs, N.J.: Prentice-Hall, 1965.

Rabi I.I. et al. *Oppenheimer*. New York: Charles Scribner's Sons, 1969.

Rhodes, Richard. *The Making of the Atomic Bomb*. New York: Simon and Schuster, 1986.

Royal, Denise. *The Story of J. Robert Oppenheimer*. New York: St. Martin's Press, 1969.

Schell, Jonathan. *The Fate of the Earth*. New York: Knopf, 1982.

Segrè, Emilio. *From X-Rays to Quarks: Modern Physicists and Their Discoveries*. New York: W.H. Freeman, 1980.

Sherwin, Martin J. *A World Destroyed: Hiroshima and the Origins of the Arms Race*. New York: Vintage Books, 1987.

Smith, Alice Kimball, and Charles Weiner, eds. *Robert Oppenheimer: Letters and Recollections*. Cambridge, Mass.: Harvard University Press, 1980.

Sommer, Mark. *Beyond the Bomb: Living Without Nuclear Weapons*. Chestnut Hill, Mass.: Expro Press, 1985.

Stimson, Henry L. "The Decision to Use the Atomic Bomb." *Harper's Magazine*, February 1947: 97–107.
Szilard, Leo. "Truman Did Not Understand." *U.S. News and World Report*, August 15, 1960: 68–69.
Teller, Edward, with Allen Brown. *The Legacy of Hiroshima*. Garden City, N.Y.: Doubleday, 1962.
Wyden, Peter. *Day One: Before Hiroshima and After*. New York: Simon and Schuster, 1984.

INDEX

Implosion bombs, 48–49
Interim Committee, 63–65, 80
International controls, 10, 60–61,
    80–81
Iwo Jima, 62

Japan
    attack by, 32, Insert 11
    cost of invading, 12
    dropping of bomb on, 69–77
    surrender of, 76–77, Insert 16
    war against, 61–68
Jewish scientists, exile of, 22–23
Joe I, 82

Kennedy, John F., 83, 88
Khrushchev, Nikita S., 83, 88
Kistiakowsky, George, 49
Kokura, Japan, 76
Kyoto, Japan, 70

Lawrence, Ernest O., 51, 63, 80
Leukemia, 75
Lilienthal, David, 10
Lindbergh, Charles A., 24
Lippmann, Walter, 83
Little Boy, 48, 68–69
    dropping of, 71–75
    reliability of, 55
Los Alamos, N.M., 9–10, 38–39,
    42–49, 79

McCarthy, Joseph, 84
MAD (mutually assured
    destruction), 85
Marshall, George C., 30, 68
Marshall, James C., 36
Matter and energy, 19
MAUD Report, 28–29, 57
Mein Kampf (Hitler), 23
Meitner, Lise, 21, Insert 7
Mental health, 15
Met Lab, 33–35

Mike, 82
Military-industrial complex, 14
Military Policy Committee, 37–38
Miller, Merle, 81

Nagasaki, Japan, 76, Insert 15
Nakamura, Hatsuyo, 72–73
Napoleon, 26
National Defense Research
    Committee, 29
Nazi Party, 9, 23, Insert 4
Neddermeyer, Seth, 48–49
Neutrons, 20–21
Newton, Isaac, 17–18
Nichols, Kenneth D., 37
Nuclear Age, 14
Nuclear Ecology Research Project,
    15
Nuclear energy, 15–16, 58–59,
    63–64
Nuclear fission, 21–30, 35
Nuclear winter, 85
Nucleus of atoms, 18

Oak Ridge, Tenn., 38, 50–54,
    Insert 10
Oliphant, Mark, 29
Oppenheimer, J. Robert, Inserts 3, 5
    on arms race, 83
    and communism, 40, 84
    as director of Los Alamos,
        39–44, 46
    and General Advisory
        Committee, 82
    and Interim Committee, 63–
        64, 80
    opposition by, 89
    and petition to FDR, 65
    at Princeton, 79
    and thermal diffusion, 53
    and Trinity test, 9, 12–13,
        55, 67
Oppenheimer, Kitty, 40, 46

★ 110 ★